Evolution of Medical Tourism:
From Cottage Industry to Corporate World

Mr. Pramod Goel – A Brief Overview

Mr. Pramod Goel is President and founder of PlacidWay, an internationally recognized industry leader in medical tourism. PlacidWay is a US-based medical tourism company with presence in over 25 countries worldwide, offering the most comprehensive solutions to over 160 medical providers globally, from India to Mexico, and Costa Rica to Ukraine.

PlacidWay's global presence includes patient referrals from all regions including North and South America, Europe, the Middle East, the CIS, Africa, and Asia. With over one million healthcare consumers from million healthcare consumers from these regions accessing PlacidWay websites annually, PlacidWay has become a tough leader in the industry, providing globally deployed industry best practices focused to attract international patients. PlacidWay has become an ultimate internet resource for the medical tourism industry.

Mr. Goel has a diverse and experience-rich background building and orchestrating start-ups, turnarounds, and growth-oriented ventures. His strategic leadership and entrepreneurship has resulted in several globally successful enterprises. He is a big picture thinker, with focus on establishing best business practices, enterprise standards, and operational excellence.

Mr. Goel has been an instrumental part of many global organizations, delivering many strategic and tactical solutions across multiple industries such as healthcare, technology, travel/hospitality, energy and manufacturing. His vast management consulting experience includes strategic planning, operational execution, and enterprise business modeling, among many other competencies and achievements.

Mr. Goel holds a Master's in Industrial and Systems Engineering and a Bachelor's in Mechanical Engineering.

Pramod Goel
President & CEO
PlacidWay
Castle Rock, Colorado, USA
Phone: +1.303.317.3607
Fax: +1.720.496.1740
Email: pgoel@placidway.com
Websites:
www.placidway.com
www.placidsolutions.com
www.placidblog.com

Table of Contents

Chapter 1:
Globalization

If you look into a definition of globalization, you will find that it means, *"merging formally separate national and international markets into one large global and interconnected marketplace"*. In our globalized era, we've seem boundaries crumbling. Borders that separate people, companies, and countries are dissolving, especially in relation to use of the Internet for business and communication needs.

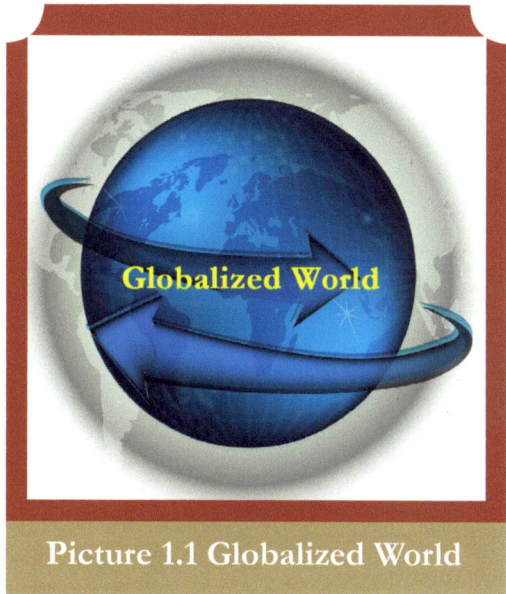

Globalized World

Picture 1.1 Globalized World

The economic (and social) impact of these separating borders literally levels the playing field for entrepreneurs and corporations around the world. Anyone can literally compete from anywhere these days.

No doubt about it, the Internet and global connection networks offer and enable untold interconnectivity than ever before. It doesn't matter if that connectivity is accessed through an iPhone, a Blackberry, a tablet, laptop or desktop computer - information, data, and money flows from country to country nearly instantly.

Products and services created and managed in one country can be delivered to another in a matter of seconds. The transfer of goods and products and services available from small or independent businesses is just as likely as from global corporations.

Add to that the ease of international travel, which is more accessible and frequent than ever before. The importance of IT technologies, communications, and social networking has promoted a truly unified global marketplace with the click of a mouse.

Global Industry Examples

Let's take just a few examples of globalization for additional perspective:

- Korean cars and television screens are consumed every where in the world.
- Chinese manufactured toys offer hours of joy to kids around the world.
- India is considered the information technology hub for the world.
- Major airlines collaborate with other world air lines to sell seats in one another's planes to utilize capacity and establish globalized networks for their customers.

It doesn't stop there. Movies and television series have taken to the global market stage as people around the world have grown fascinated with Hollywood movies, Bollywood movies, Korean soap operas, Latin music, among others.

What we're seeing is a major transition from a segmented marketplace to a HUGE marketplace.

Manufacturing - Korean cars, Tvs; Chinese toys, Electronics

Information Technology - India taking a lead role in IT

Energy - Middle East oil being consumed globally

Hospitality / Travel & Tourism - code sharing to gain competitive advantage

Entertainment - Korean Soaps, Hollywood, Bollywood

Healthcare - medical tourism the new future in healthcare

Picture 1.2 Examples of Globalized Industries

The key to these globalized industries is that people are more intercon-nected. Supply chain processes are broken down in smaller manage-able way. Well-planned distribution network systems have propelled these industries for consumers around the world. We've even begun seeing a transition in healthcare sector. Medical tourism is propelling inhabitants from around the world to break down barriers and make healthcare globally accessible, available, feasible and affordable – for everyone.

Globalization of Healthcare Industry

From a globalization perspective, where is the healthcare industry go-ing? When we talk about medical tourism as a global phenomenon, we typically think about medical treatments such as cosmetic surgeries, dental treatment, organ transplants, cardiac care or spine surgeries. We don't tend to think about other potential opportunities that present equally big opportunities.

As we live in a 'shrinking world', we're seeing a major impact on other medical related fields in addition to direct health care services, includ-ing:

- Durable medical equipment
- Consumable medical supplies
- Medical staffing needs
- Learning and education opportunities
- Clinical trials
- Pharmaceuticals

For example, we're seeing an increase in demand not only for highly trained physicians and surgeons, but also highly qualified nursing staff and customer service, non-medical and support staff.

Highly specialized medical equipment manufactured in country X is being used in medical tourism destinations around the globe, providing equal opportunities and access to care and removing concerns about technology as a differentiator when it comes to health care services. People from Iraq are going to other countries to get better trained so that they can bring those skills back to their country and treat local patients. The same occurs in countries around the world, from Turkey to South Africa to Singapore and Croatia.

In summary, as the healthcare industry continues to become more globalized, more medical related and medical and/or healthcare support fields will also become global and grow along with them. Opportunities will go beyond medical treatment and morph into a truly boundary-less system.

The Scope of Medical Tourism Today

The scope of medical tourism sources today touches a number of di-fferent areas within the health and wellness industry.

• *Medical Services* – Access to doctors and surgeons for a variety of treatments and procedures, diagnostics and imaging services globally.

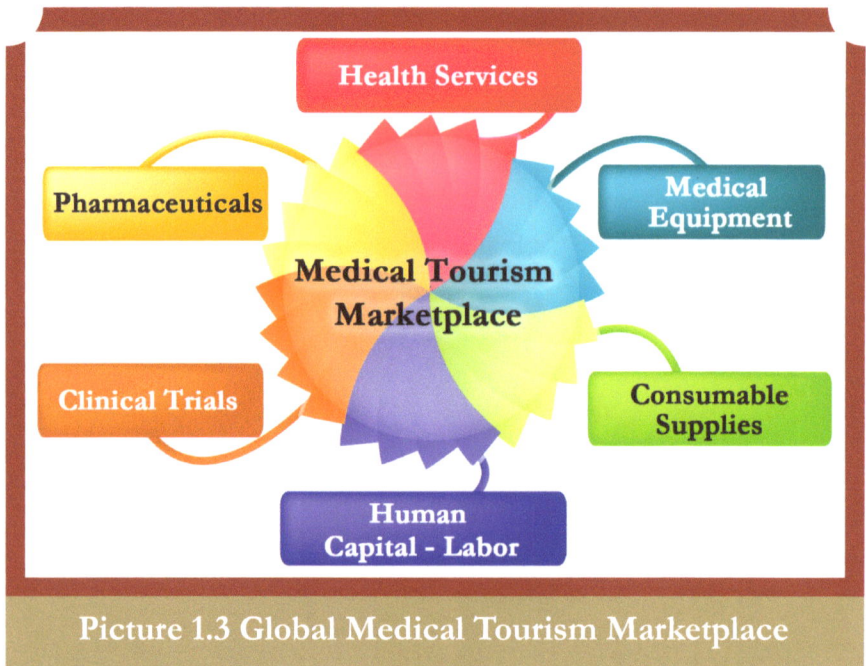

Picture 1.3 Global Medical Tourism Marketplace

- *Health & Wellness Services* – From well-checks to prenatal care to hospice care, individuals are seeking well-rounded programs offering health and wellness programs (including preventive care services) from A to Z.

-

  Medical Equipment – Durable and consumable medical equipment, tools and gadgets, goods and supplies, from blood glucose monitors to home healthcare aides are increasing in demand.

- *Education* – Higher degrees, continuing education, certification and on-site and off-site training programs for specialties and focused care is on the rise.

- *Medical Services* – Access to doctors and surgeons for a variety of treatments and procedures, diagnostics and imaging services globally.

- *Health & Wellness Services* – From well-checks to prenatal care to hospice care, individuals are seeking well-rounded programs offering health and wellness programs (including preventive care services) from A to Z.

- *Medical Equipment* – Durable and consumable medical equipment, tools and gadgets, goods and supplies, from blood glucose monitors to home healthcare aides are increasing in demand.

- *Education* – Higher degrees, continuing education, certification and on-site and off-site training programs for specialties and focused care is on the rise.

- *Labor force* - e.g., An increased demand for trained nursing staff, highly qualified doctors, experienced and certified surgeons, facilities and support staff to maintain such facilities.

- *Clinical Trials* – New drugs and treatments (including stem cell technologies) continue to expand treatment and therapy horizons.

- *Pharmaceuticals* – Countries around the world develop new drugs and medications every day.

Globalization Influencers

What are the main influences that drive globalization? A handful of influences have an impact on any market. For example:

Economics – The economics of a solution drives people to think differently. In the case of healthcare globalization, economics are considered one of the top reasons a consumer makes one choice or decision over another.

Cultures – We were previously bound by cultural boundaries, but as we move forward as a global society, these cultural boundaries are shrinking. As we say in America, cultures around the world today are a literal "melting pot". Different cultures are blending knowledge and awareness of each other, compelling people to integrate, adapt and accept different perceptions and approaches to life.

Specialization – Medical solutions today are increasingly specialized, which offers an increased depth of knowledge in one area and more tangible results. For example, a cancer specialization facility or doctor who sees thousands of cases of cancer a year can present better outcomes than a physician who sees only ten cases a year. As the globalization in healthcare flourishes, this field will increase and people will see a definite increase in specialized treatments.

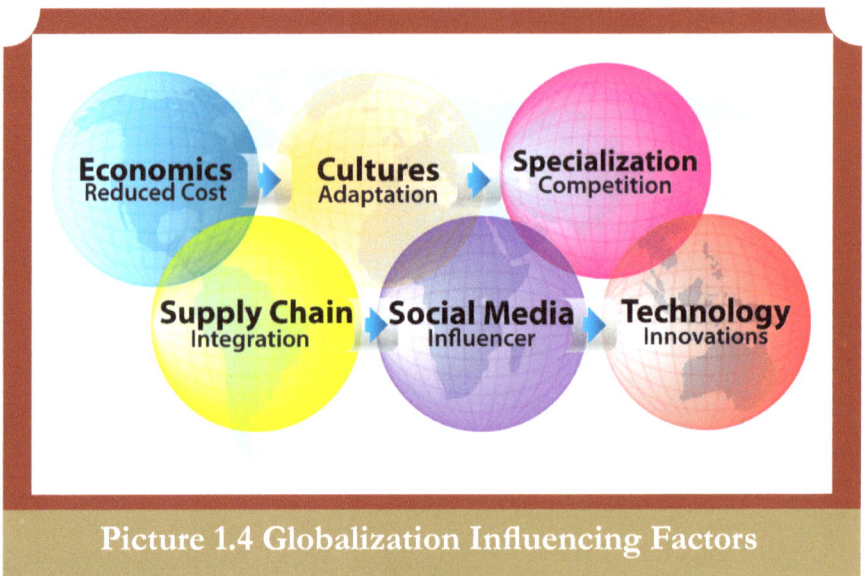

Economics Reduced Cost
Cultures Adaptation
Specialization Competition
Supply Chain Integration
Social Media Influencer
Technology Innovations

Picture 1.4 Globalization Influencing Factors

Supply Chain – The integration of one's supply chain has been one of the most important factors in any successful industry that has gone global. Whenever the pieces of the supply chain are properly understood and coordinated, the results are astronomical. A well-planned and working supply chain improves the business processes and reduces waste from the system and hence optimizes overall results.

Social Media - In today's society, social media is one of those elements that has become key factor of removing economic, cultural, religious barriers. This is a segment of any successful business that can't be ignored as they key influencer in your success.

Technology – The continuous evolution in technology has propelled the healthcare system into new heights. With right technologies in place, same solutions (and synchronization inpatient care processes) can be available anywhere in the world.

Is Medical Tourism a Huge Opportunity?

So now, we have a question in front of us. How big is medical tourism? Is this a great opportunity in globalized health care system?

There are various financial considerations regarding the number of people expected to travel under the global healthcare or medical tourism umbrella in coming years. Some estimates refer to a $100 billion industry with over 40 million people traveling around the world for healthcare. No matter how you look at the industry, it continues to grow and become a mainstream phenomenon.

It is significantly big enough to compel us to understand it better. It is complex enough to get lost in the mayhem of information, trends, cultures, competition, and realty versus myths.

America used to be considered the ultimate as a big target market for inbound medical tourism. Is this still a true phenomenon? It's not an easy answer, but let's just say that numerous doctors, surgeons, clinics and hospital facilities around the globe are giving the U.S. a run for its money, and for a lot less of it – while still adhering, and surpassing international standards of care and quality.

So which countries are emerging in the field of medical tourism? While India and Thailand gained initial traction of becoming market leaders, a rise of regional solutions have emerged, capturing and expanding the market reach.

For example, South Korea started making inroads with CIS, Russia, China and far-east Asian markets, while Turkey being very strategically situated in the middle of the world is increasing becoming a destination of choice for middle easterners as well as for medical travelers from CIS (Commonwealth of Independent States) and Europeans. In Latin America, Mexico and Costa Rica continue to lead the charge while Colombia is emerging as a strong contender in the Latin American market.

We have to also realize that in this BIG industry, there is a HUGE competition as well. As we understand it, over 60 countries are trying to compete with a wide variety of products and services. Over 40,000 medical service providers offer "same services" in this industry. All these service providers are trying to tap into the same pool of potential medical travelers.

So how do you compete? This brings us to a point of whenever there is an opportunity, there are problems that must be addressed and should be considered in designing the solution for next generation to evolve.

First we need to understand several myths in the medical tourism industry.
For example:

• Most Americans are traveling to Asian countries such as India for medical treatment. In fact, what we are observing is the trend that most Americans will consider traveling to Latin America before considering far Asian or Eastern European destinations due to cost, distance/flight time, time lost, familiarity of a culture, among other things.

• Medical Tourism is a new phenomenon. In fact, medical travel has been a global phenomenon for decades as people travel from one country to other for medical treatment. However, it is perhaps a newer concept in America.

• Only uninsured Americans travel abroad for medical care. In fact, the uninsured do not travel abroad for medical care, as they do not have the necessary funds for the out-of-pocket treatment. The insured with high deductibles, the self-insured, and people with discretionary income are the most common travelers for medical care.

• When people travel abroad for medical care, they only look for JCI (Joint Commissions International) accredited hospitals and facilities. In fact, consumers traveling for healthcare rarely know what JCI is, and only a small fraction of medical travelers are aware of such international accreditation.

- When people are looking abroad for medical care, their main concern is quality. In fact, when people are traveling their main concern is cost and quality, and in most cases, quality is **assumed** to be available.

Medical Tourism Industry Challenges

We'll break this section down so you can view it at a glance. We'll cover these topics more fully throughout this book. However, to get us started, let's look at some of the issues and challenges prevalent in today's medical tourism industry.

Competition – Local, Regional and Global Levels:

Local doctors and hospitals have relooked into their services and cost offerings and begun providing a competitive product in the marketplace – a price point that is growingly more aligned, considering global competition. From a medical tourism perspective, doctors and hospitals offering similar services are trying to attract the medical tourist with similar propositions. As the awareness and potential of this industry grows, many local providers are considering and participating in the marketplace, making it a highly competitive marketplace. These local doctors and hospitals are growing smarter and gaining better trained from international accredited bodies in order to compete in the global economy.

For example, doctors within America are reducing their pricing and increasing their value proposition to retain their customers. Doctors and hospitals in Mexico or India or Turkey are competing with one another to gain their market share in the medical tourism industry. Hence, local level competition within a country increases.

Regional level competition is growing as number of countries are supporting and encouraging its healthcare and tourism resources to attract healthcare tourist as a new channel of income to propel regional economy. Within Latin America, we see solutions emerging from Mexico to Costa Rica to Colombia, and from Argentina to Brazil, and list continues to grow with new entrants in the marketplace. Each country within the region tries to attract a similar client base and hence makes the market over crowded with little or no distinction in value proposition.

At a **global level,** competition is becoming more prominent. Various major countries are "trying" to offer a product to the medical tourism market, which often again hinges upon cost, quality and service. For example, India's main value proposition was cost, Thailand's as a tourist destination, and Germany's was superior quality. As the competition at global levels increases, these distinctions and value propositions are blurring and the original perceived competitive edge has diminished.

More Supply than Demand

As we discussed earlier, over 60 countries are competing with over 40,000 medical service providers. This creates a situation of more supply than current industry demand. There are limited efforts to increase the awareness that will propel additional demand. With significant imbalance between supply and demand has resulted in price war.

Economic Situation

In order to reach supply-demand equilibrium, we have to understand the worldwide medical tourism market's specific needs and develop customized solutions instead of continuing to rely on "one size fits all" type of solution. The new innovative solutions and awareness of global healthcare options in the marketplace is the only way we can propel more demand to meet the existing supply.

The worldwide economic situation has a dramatic impact on the Medical Tourism industry. The industrialized nation has seen overall declines in income levels or increasing unemployment, which influences citizens to avoid spending money for elective procedures. Decreased discretionary income has resulted in decreased demand for medical procedures that are elective or critical in general, as people are delaying/postponing receiving desired treatment. Economic pressures have caused people to be more careful with their discretionary income.

On the other hand, the rise in economic status in certain regions such as Asia has created a new market for people seeking high-end, best-of-the-best procedures abroad. The demand from this region continues to grow as the economic status of people here has dramatically changed in last decade and continues to evolve.

Rapid Rise in Local, Regional & Global Competition

More Supply than Demand

Reliability on World Economy

Unsustainable Medical Tourism Business Models

Unstructured Market Approaches

Customer Needs Focused Solutions

Picture 1.5 Medical Tourism Marketing Challenges

Sustainable Business Models

With the rapid rise in Medical Tourism industry in last ten years or so, the market has seen too many business models that are unrealistic and unsustainable at this time.

With limited knowledge of business fundamentals, several medical and service providers have adopted old and archaic solutions. These business solutions are designed to earn quick income rather than creating a sustainable business opportunity for the long term. With lack of sustainable infrastructure and associated business foundation and fundamentals, the industry is unable to take the leap into next generation.

What is the Future of Global Healthcare Industry?

So where is this industry going – is this still a viable option?

As defined by Geoffrey Moore in a book titled, "Crossing the Chasm," all disruptive technologies goes through a product cycle will have a chasm – and lot of companies trying to compete in that marketplace will fall into that chasm.

We consider that the medical tourism industry is currently going through that phase and is well into the 'chasm'. The big market still exists, but we are at a tip of the iceberg and only a partial solution has been developed. We have to move from the early market to mainstream market customer base, which is much bigger and requires a more structured approach to the industry.

This mature global healthcare market would demand a perfect solution – not a broken system. It would require people to provide a price point that is globally competitive so that each consumer has ability to buy that product anywhere.

It would require brand establishment, as well as complete transparency. In order to compete in the future global healthcare market, we must think differently.

The ideal solution has not yet been discovered, but we should all think about a new era, which provides more insights on the supply chain of what we are working toward. It doesn't matter whether it's a clinic seeking patients from abroad or you're providing coordination services for patients traveling from one country to another, or whether you're a medical equipment manufacturer looking into new distribution channels.

We must innovate and rethink on the industry. We must realize where we have been and focus on where we want to go. This can be achieved only through understanding fundamentals of business, such as your own supply chain, and your own distribution strategy.

For this we must align our people, processes and systems to identify what, who, why, when, how to grow the business across international boundaries.

Chapter 2:
Future of Global
Healthcare Industry

The future of global healthcare is still evolving. Even with current industry challenges of delivering (and at times, the inability to deliver) medical services to millions of people traveling for medical reasons, the industry still has the potential of surpassing any historical predictions. The three-dimensional ability of medical providers around the globe to provide such services offers the field a game-changing industry in this formerly, two-dimensional, flat world.

New trends are still evolving… the key factors of new medical tourism era will depend on how we adopt to a changing world. Before we adopt and understand the future, we need to see how this industry mirrors other industries. We need to understand how the evolution of technology industry, travel and tourism industry, entertainment industry or even a manufacturing industry followed a path quite similar to

the one are currently undertaking.

Each of these industries went through an evolutionary process – rising sharply, falling through the cracks, and then rising again to become a main street market. The medical tourism industry also showed a significant potential early on, based on "presumed" industry needs. Today, the medical tourism industry is going through a phase where we see "industry", and are therefore trying to figure out what the actual need of the industry is, and how to serve those healthcare consumer needs in the most appropriate way.

In order to understand the future of medical tourism industry, we need to:

• Understand the evolution of any product lifecycle – the phases any new product development and it's growth rely on - including changes.

- We need to evaluate the famous "chasm theory" and see how the medical tourism industry mirrors this market phenomenon.

- We need to understand the product evolution phases necessary for this market-

- We need to evaluate the characteristics of a market leader to lead this industry.

- We need to understand the key factors that one must consider to survive and thrive.

- Finally, we need to understand the value chain of the medical tourism market.

The key components of the foundation will be to have the right people, the right processes, and the right systems in place. A successful program in future will include these three components wor-king in tandem. In order to achieve this understanding, we must align:

- **People**
- **Processes**
- **Systems**

Only by doing so will we be able to identify what, who, why, when, and how to grow the business across international boundaries in this globalized and highly competitive economy.

Understanding the Medical Tourism Chasm

The progression of medical tourism in recent decades is a classical theory that was presented by renowned writer, Geoffrey Moore in his book, "Cross this Chasm". Every industry goes through a product development lifecycle from early adoption to the mainstream market before it is replaced by next "new" phenomena. A "chasm" is a gap between two things – it could be profound differences between people, viewpoints, interests, feelings, or loyalty.

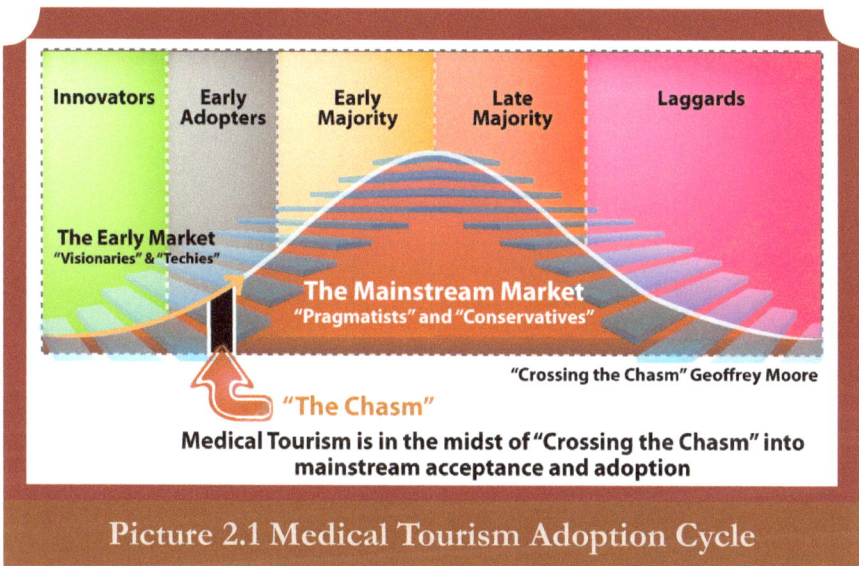

Picture 2.1 Medical Tourism Adoption Cycle

However, before the transition happens, from early adopters to the mainstream market, many revolutionary technologies goes through a "gulf" or as defined by Geoffrey Moore, a "chasm".

Only companies understanding the characteristics of the mainstream market are able to successfully cross the chasm. Many companies seeking to make a "quick buck" based on early market adopters fall into this chasm and are unable to get out of it.

The medical tourism industry is also currently going through this phase and in the "chasm". It has not crossed the chasm to reach out to the mainstream market, which is significantly large and would require more innovations and structure to win the health care consumers.

We're at the tip of the iceberg however, and only a partial solution has been developed.

We have to move from 'early' market to 'main stream' market, which, while bigger, also requires a more structured approach to the overall industry.

Early Medical Tourism Adopter Market ▬

The early market adopters of medical tourism accepted incomplete solutions. Characteristics of people who reached out to seek medical tourism experience thus far include:

- 80% or partial solution is acceptable
- Aggressively pursue new ways to solve problems
- They're not seeking full justification for their international travel needs
- Looking for setting initial industry trends

Take, for example, this story of an early-market adopter:

Johnny, age 32, is a well-educated, techno enthusiast looking for knee surgery due to an injury caused by an active lifestyle. During his youth, he was an aggressive athlete, and injured his knees. Despite his youth, he now needs a knee replacement, which is not covered by his insurance plan. Through research, he found the solution across the globe, but some aspects of his surgery were not ideal. He had to take unpaid time off work; the doctor at the facility was not renowned in his field.

It's hard to find perfect conditions for anything, let alone a surgical procedure in another country. However, he felt prepared to take any procedure, as he wanted to aggressively pursue treatment and a solution for his problem. Even though the solution was not ideal and addressed only 80% of his needs, he was ready to take the risk. He didn't care about the rest - he was used to living in a cutting edge environment. He went across the globe and obtained his surgery for less money, and the procedure provided the same good outcome as it would have been at his hometown hospital.

Characteristics of Early Adopters
Opinion Leaders

Johnny is what we call an early adopter, or opinion leader. He shows these types of characteristics:

- **Innovative** – He's proactive, researching and learning on his own what he wants.
- **Technically Competent** – He's capable of searching out and finding solutions anywhere, not limiting himself to local resources.
- **Socially Accessible** – He liked the idea of visiting another country.
- **Higher media exposure** - Social media brought the world to Johnny's fingertips.
- **Customer Value** – Benefits - Price - He received the same treatment and procedure as he would have at his own hospital, though for lot less money, which was one of the main drivers for his initiatives.
- **Risk takers** – accepts broken solutions - Sure, Johnny would have loved to have been able to receive his surgery at home, but it was too expensive, as his insurance didn't provide for such coverage.

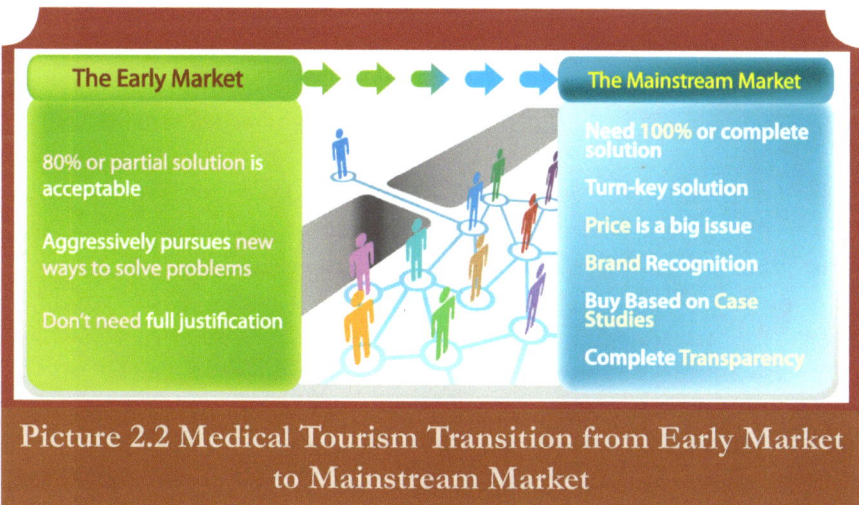

The Early Market

80% or partial solution is acceptable

Aggressively pursues new ways to solve problems

Don't need full justification

The Mainstream Market

Need 100% or complete solution

Turn-key solution

Price is a big issue

Brand Recognition

Buy Based on Case Studies

Complete Transparency

Picture 2.2 Medical Tourism Transition from Early Market to Mainstream Market

Main Stream Medical Tourism Market

A mature global healthcare market demands a perfect solution, not a broken system, not an 80% solution. A mature global healthcare market also requires individuals to provide globally competitive price points so that a consumer has ability to buy that product anywhere. A mature global healthcare market would require:

- **Global Brands:** An established brand recognition which projects trust.
- **Complete Solution**: a solution that addresses all related issues.
- **Transparency**: no hidden costs, no hidden unethical techniques.
- **Price**: this will be a key factor.
- **Quality**: proven and demonstrable quality through customer experience.
- **Review**: based on peer-to-peer reviews.

In order to compete in the future global healthcare market we must think differently. The ideal solution for ultimate success has not yet been discovered. Still, we all need to think about a new era that provides more insights on the supply chain of what we're working toward. This applies to a clinic-seeking patients from abroad to buyers seeking to coordinate patients from one country to another, to medical equipment manufacturers looking into wider distribution channels.

We must be innovative and rethink the industry. We need to understand where it has been, but more importantly, where we can take this industry. Doing so can only be achieved by understanding some basic fundamentals clearly. Such fundamentals include understanding your own supply chain and distribution strategy.

Here's another example, this time focusing on the 'Main Stream Market Consumer':

Suzanne, aged 64, is a conservative buyer. Although she has limited funds and no insurance, she wants, and is willing, to take time to understand solutions to her problems that she is seeking. She's cautious and careful. She'll think long and hard before making any decision. She's looking for a perfect solution that meets her specific needs and desires. Her cautious buying behavior is looking for a "proven" solution. She does not live on the edge.

She needs to be fully convinced before she decides to go abroad for surgical reasons.

Her buying characteristics include:

- Needs 100% or complete solution
- Looking for turn-key solutions
- Price is a big issue
- Seeking brand recognition
- Buy based on case studies
- Complete transparency

Suzanne is a typical consumer for the mainstream market.

Main Stream Marketing Characteristics

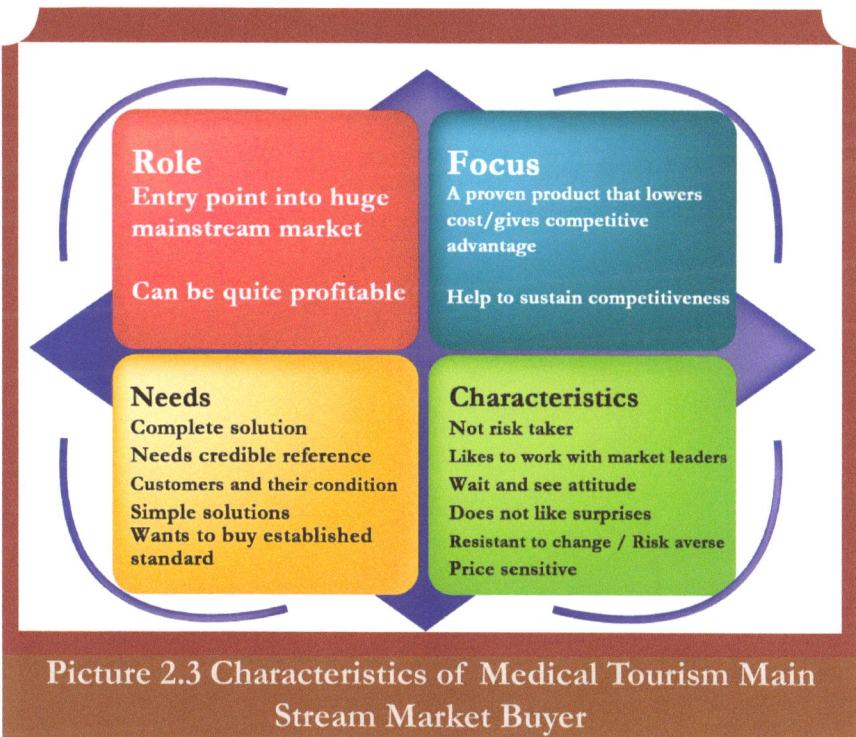

Role
Entry point into huge mainstream market

Can be quite profitable

Focus
A proven product that lowers cost/gives competitive advantage

Help to sustain competitiveness

Needs
Complete solution
Needs credible reference
Customers and their condition
Simple solutions
Wants to buy established standard

Characteristics
Not risk taker
Likes to work with market leaders
Wait and see attitude
Does not like surprises
Resistant to change / Risk averse
Price sensitive

Picture 2.3 Characteristics of Medical Tourism Main Stream Market Buyer

People like Suzanne offer the following characteristics when looking for their medical solutions. They're:

- Practical people.
- Do not follow trends/fads.
- Make cautious buying decisions.
- Buy based on well-established references.
- Follow established purchasing standards.

It's important to understand the characteristics of your potential customers. If you don't know them, you don't know which approach to marketing to use that best meets their needs. Understanding the differences of approach, from an early-market adopter to a mainstream buyer, of a 30-year-old to a 65-year-old when it comes to marketing your services can make all the difference in the world.

Learn to recognize and acknowledge this difference or "chasm" that differentiates them from one another. Yes, they're both looking for solutions, but they're going at it in different ways. Your ability to cater to such different approaches will distinguish you in this competitive field.

Crossing the Chasm Requires a Shift in Delivered Values:

In order to cross the medical tourism chasm, to move from early adopter market to mainstream markets, we must:

- Focus on product/services centric values
- We must think about what distinguishes us from the rest.
- Do our products and/or services offer a unique value proposition?

Meeting the needs of the "main street" market and aligning the solutions around their specific needs, characteristics of the market allows us to distinguish ourselves in the marketplace and provide us a cutting-edge solution.

Remember, you must be able to identify and recognize the "chasm". As mentioned earlier, the chasm is that point in between an 'early adopter' type of customer market and a 'mainstream' customer market. Think of this "chasm" as a gorge or gully that your business must bridge or span in order to benefit from early development to full-fledged mainstream market benefits. Don't worry so much about making that 'quick buck', but focus on your profits and growth over the long haul.

One way you can bridge the chasm or gorge is through leadership, and that also includes market leadership.

Medical Tourism Leadership

So, it is great that we live in a globalized world. Healthcare is also becoming globalized. The future of this global healthcare is vast but not easy – we need to innovate within the sector – so how do we compete?

Based on the book, "The Disciplines of Market Leaders," by Treacy & Wiersema, one of the ways to compete in this industry is to identify what you are good at. In order to rise above the competition and to capture leadership position in the mainstream market, we have to understand clearly our own value proposition. We need to identify our niche so that we can continue to hone and address a specific consumer need.

We can't be everything to everyone. Remember when we discussed specialization? Not everyone can do everything. You have to find your own niche, whether you're receiving patients from the global marketplace OR facilitating patients from your own country.

Key Factors of Survival in Global Healthcare Industry

According to Treacy & Wiersema, there are three key factors to survival in today's global healthcare industry. These include:

Healthcare Leadership – Are you presenting a unique healthcare solution for your clients? Will people pay a premium for this solution e.g., stem cell therapy or advanced cancer treatments. Do you have a situation where either there are not many solutions available, or you're among the top providers in the world providing this solution? **Product innovation** is the key factor for this category.

Customer Intimacy – How close you can get with a customer to gain their trust? Are you able to provide complete turnkey medical tourism solutions to your customers? How far are you willing to go to delight your customers? **Service** is the key factor for this category.

Healthcare Leadership

Forefront of innovation in healthcare, e.g., stem cell, cancer, orthopedic and integrative medicine.

Products and services that are innovative & distinct – time to market and results are important.

Customer Intimacy

Attend to every detail of healthcare tourists - build trusted relationships and an exceptional experience and know the people you sell to.

Personal service that builds trusted relationships – service and long-term relations are key attributes.

Operational Excellence

Specific expertise combined with unbeatable price, quality, and ease of purchase.

Quality, selection, timing and unbeatable prices are key attributes for the smart shopper.

Picture 2.4 Characteristics of Medical Tourism Market Leaders

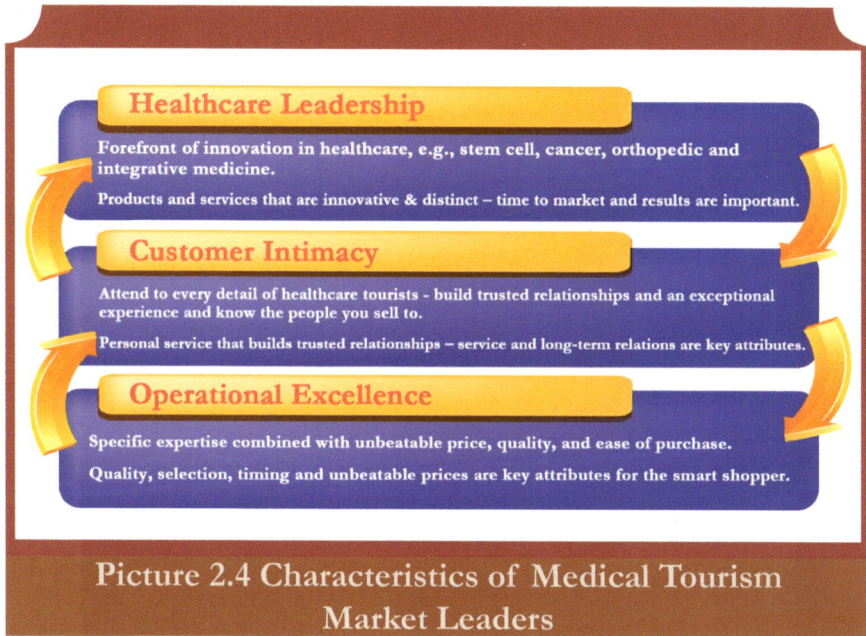

Operational Excellence – Is your business process completely optimized so that you can provide a lowest cost medical tourism solution without compromising quality? **Cost** is the key element for this category.

Healthcare Leadership:

Be an innovation leader when it comes to healthcare. For example, be a leader/provider in stem cell research and technology, cancer research, treatments and procedures, orthopedic research, treatments and procedures and/or integrative medicine methodologies.

Leadership in medical tourism industry will be claimed by people or organizations that prepare their unique products and services that innovate and redefine healthcare options. Innovative medical tourism product and/or service marketability and capitalization are key to successfully gaining the market share. The product and service uniqueness and ability to solve the people healthcare needs which no one else can is the main characteristic of maintaining a product leadership.

Key Points of Best Brand / Product:

- Time: timing of the solution introduction in the market place
- Functionality: key features which are not delivered by any solution in the industry
- Brand: recognizable and trusted brand which links to innovations

Case Study: Product Leadership

• Organizational Background:

- **•Treatment:** Stem Cell, Integrative Cancer Treatment, Oxinium Knee Surgery
- Geographical Target: North America, Latin America
- Demographics:
    - Age Range: 40 – 70
    - Audience: Baby boomer, men & women, educated
    - Reason: Chronic problems, unavailability of the treatment locally, awareness of global innovations

• Customer Value Proposition:

- Characteristics: time and functionality; creating best product or service;
- Breakthrough product development and execution; expectation management

• Marketing Strategy:

- Channels: Online Research, Medical Referral, Word of Mouth, Associations
- Message: What are your defensible results? How will you solve patient's problems? How fast you can demonstrate the results? How will your brand be perceived?

- **Marketing Channel Focus:**

  - Online – SEO, SEM, SMM
  - Channel Partnerships – Like-condition associations
  - Viral Marketing – seeking early adopters to rely the message

- **Marketing Materials:**

  - Patient educational materials – techniques, risks, benefits of the treatment, comparison of procedures, compari son of technology, e.g., adult stem cell vs. placenta implants

  - Patient Testimonials - well composed past patient stories for each condition treated – video and written, availability of patients for peer discussions
  - Time line to success, hope, clinical data

- **Turn-key Solution:**

  - Human Touch – personalized service
  - Convenience – all information readily available
  - Customization – customized treatment plans for each cus-tomer

Customer Intimacy:

The customer intimacy is defined in medical tourism field as a concept where you attend to every detail of medical tourists. You must build trusted relationships and create an exceptional experience for your customers. Knowing your customers specific needs, behaviors, and most importantly expectations is the focus.

The more personalized services that can be offered to build a trusted relationship with medical traveler, the better opportunity you have to distinguish yourself in the market. Excellent service, combined with service quality and long-term relationship with the prospective customer is the key to creating long-term, and repeatable and sustainable business opportunity.

Key Points of Best Service:

* Service: unparalleled service in the industry
* Long term customer relationship: trusted relationship with the patients
* Brand: recognizable and trusted brand which links to innovations

Case Study: Customer Intimacy

• Organizational Background:

- • Treatment: Multi-specialty Hospital, Orthopedic, Neuro, Heart, Cancer, General Surgery
- • Geographical Target: North America, Latin America
- • Demographics:
  - • Age Range: 22 – 65; 22-35 years with limited medical benefits
  - • Audience: Baby boomer, both men and women; un-insured, self-insured, self-insured companies
  - • Reason: Cost, long lead time, experience/second opinion

• Customer Value Proposition:

- • Characteristics: service, trusted relationship
- • Personalized service, dependability, measurable outcomes, convenience

• Marketing Strategy:

- • Channels: Online, Insurance, Medical Referral, Word of Mouth, Associations
- • Message: What is your total solution? How will you solve patient's specific problems? Do you understand Personas of your customers? Do you customize your solution for each individual?

• Channel Focus:

- • Online – SEO, SEM, SMM
- • Channels – Insurance, Medical Referrals

• Marketing Materials:

- • Solutions Development – comprehensive solution offerings, value added services
- • Patient educational materials – techniques, risks, benefits of the treatment, comparison of procedures, comparison of technology
- • Patient Testimonials - well composed past patient stories showing compassion and faith in your services – video and written
- • Local, regional, international, product/ price comparison

• Turn-key Solution:

- • Human Touch – personalized and trusted relationship
- • Convenience – being patient guide
- • Customization – Market of "One"; completely customized solution

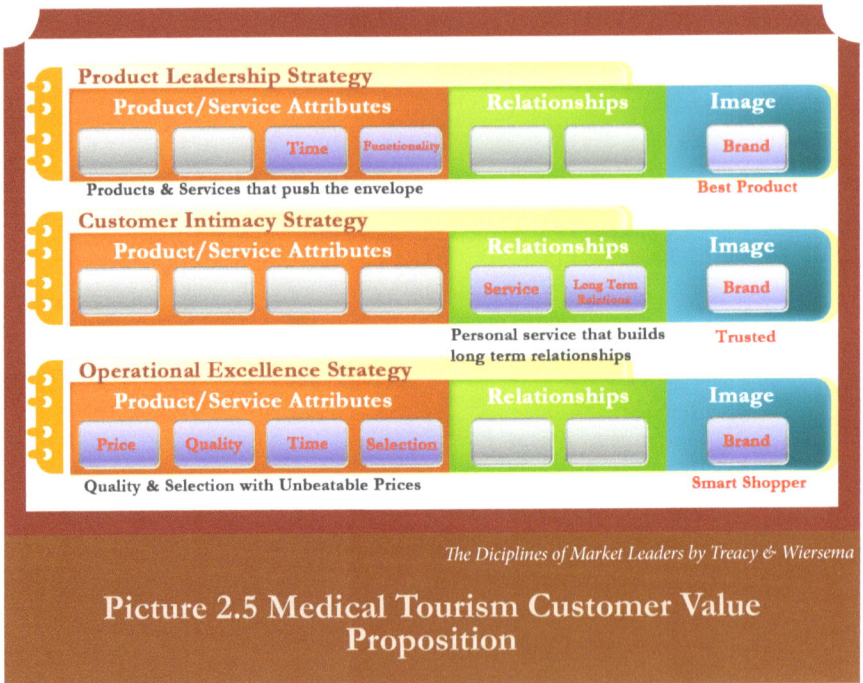

Product Leadership Strategy

Product/Service Attributes				Relationships		Image
		Time	Functionality			Brand

Products & Services that push the envelope — Best Product

Customer Intimacy Strategy

Product/Service Attributes				Relationships		Image
				Service	Long Term Relations	Brand

Personal service that builds long term relationships — Trusted

Operational Excellence Strategy

Product/Service Attributes				Relationships		Image
Price	Quality	Time	Selection			Brand

Quality & Selection with Unbeatable Prices — Smart Shopper

The Diciplines of Market Leaders by Treacy & Wiersema

Picture 2.5 Medical Tourism Customer Value Proposition

Operational Excellence

Operational excellence in medical tourism industry relates to offering specific expertise combined with unbeatable price, quality, and ease of purchase. The medical tourism providers must offer a top-notch quality, multiple selections and options, best availability and timing, combined with unbeatable prices. These are the key attributes of an operationally excellent organization, which a smart shopper will look for.

Key Points of Best Service:
- Price: Lowest price in the local area or industry
- Quality: good quality
- Time: lead time to procure the product is very low
- Brand: smart shopper

Case Study: Operational Excellence

• Organizational Background:

- **Treatment**: Dental, Cosmetics, Fertility, Lasik
- Geographical Target: North America, Latin America
- Demographics:
- Age Range: 35– 65
- Audience: Baby boomer, Female, Medium to High Income
- Reason: improved appearance, active life, enjoys trends, experience and indulgence

• Customer Value Proposition:

- Characteristics: price, quality, time and selection
- Quality and selection with unbeatable price

• Marketing Strategy:

- Channels: Online, Physical Channels, Print, Word of Mouth
- Message: What is your unique value proposition? How will your brand be perceived? How will you make patient feel special? Will you able to provide the best costs that combine all elements?

• Channel Focus:

- Online – SEO, SEM, SMM
- Tourism Services Referrals & Packaging – hotels, spas

• Marketing Materials:

- Patient educational materials – techniques, risks, benefits of the treatment, comparison of procedure A vs. B, comparison of technology, e.g., Nobel BioCare vs. Zimmer implants
- Compelling all-inclusive package integration
- Well composed past patient stories for each condition treated
- Price comparison chart, local, regional, international, product price comparison

Medical Tourism Customer Value Proposition Exercise

How do you believe your company approaches the marketplace?
What is your customer's perception your company?
How do you differentiate from your competition?

(Specify key attributes that support your customer value proposition)

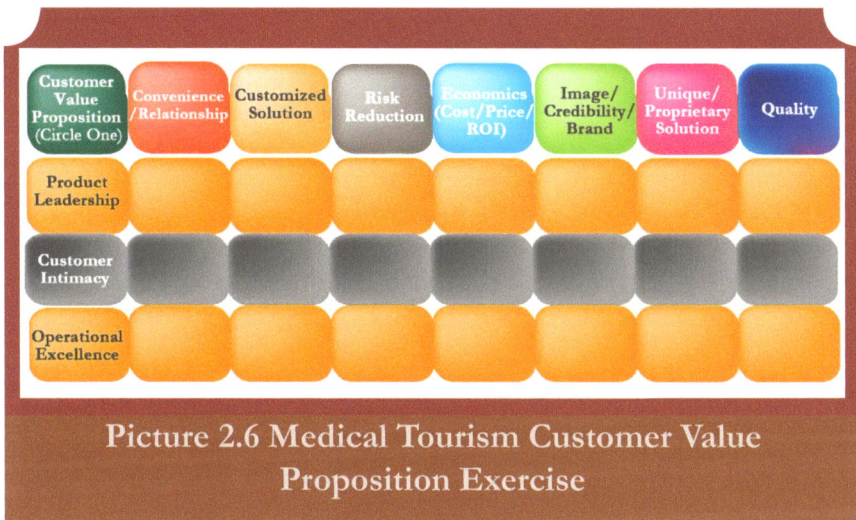

Customer Value Proposition (Circle One)	Convenience /Relationship	Customized Solution	Risk Reduction	Economics (Cost/Price/ ROI)	Image/ Credibility/ Brand	Unique/ Proprietary Solution	Quality
Product Leadership							
Customer Intimacy							
Operational Excellence							

Picture 2.6 Medical Tourism Customer Value Proposition Exercise

Customer Value Proposition Definitions

- **Product Leadership –** The Company is a producer of leading-edge products & services. Intel, Apple, and Boeing are examples. Products and services that push the envelope – time-to-market and product functionality are key attributes.

- **Customer Intimacy –** An enterprise that builds bonds with its customers and knows the people it sells to. British Air and Home Depot are examples. Personal service that builds trusted relationship – service and long-term relations are key attributes.

- **Operational Excellence –** An organization focused on delivering quality, price, and ease of purchase. Costco and Southwest Air are examples. Quality, selection, timing and unbeatable price are key attributes for smart shopper.

Medical Tourism Sustainability Program

Once you have realized the characteristics of mainstream markets and its consumer behavior as well as your specific consumer value proposition as a key selling points, then you have to figure out how you're going to develop a sustainable medical tourism business to capture your targeted marketplace.

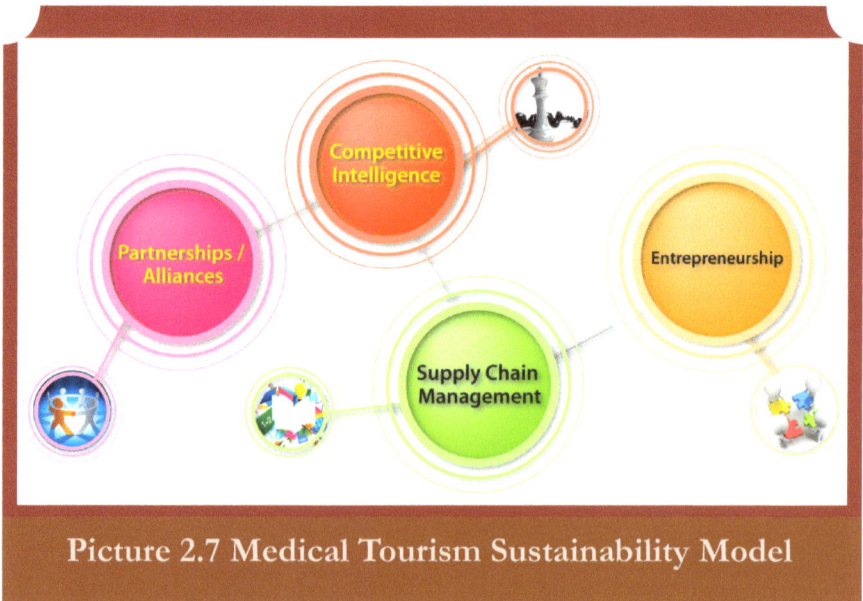

Picture 2.7 Medical Tourism Sustainability Model

Following each of these guidelines, you'll have a greater chance of success. In order to successfully compete in the global market, you must be able to create an infrastructure that forms a solid foundation of your program.

The key elements in developing a sustainable business include:

- Partnerships and Alliances
- Competitive Intelligence
- Supply Chain Management
- Entrepreneurship

We'll break each of the above down a little more for additional clarity.

Partnerships and Alliances:

Partnerships and alliances are one way to expand in the medical tourism market. Leverage your relationships with key players such as equipment manufacturers, pharmaceutical industry reps, local doctors, insurance agents, and medical tourism facilitators, among others in target markets. These are representatives from various medical market segmentations who can provide local targeted market intelligence to help you establish your product and services abroad.

Competitive Intelligence:

Competitive intelligence involves understanding your specific competitive edge. For example, how you will compete and on what basis? Understanding your local, regional, and global competition is essential in developing products and services that can distinguish you in this highly competitive marketplace.

Supply Chain Management:

Understanding supply chain management is the key to any industry's sustainable growth. Supply chain management in medical tourism industry relates to the manage ment of a network of interconnected businesses involved in the provision of medical services and packages needed by the end consumers.

The management of the process also includes designing, planning, execution, control and monitoring of the supply chain activities with the objective of creating net value, building foundation and infrastructure, logistics management, while aligning supply and demand and measuring key performance criteria established. Supply Chain management is defined as understanding and optimizing your supply chain management systems, including your 'touch points' for patients.

Entrepreneurship:

As with any new growth industry, the medical tourism industry has been propelled by entrepreneurs. As we go forward, these entrepreneurs need to continue to undertake innovations, finance, and business acumen in an effort to transform medical tourism concepts into economic success for all. The innovations by these entrepreneurs and intrapreneurship will help this industry to move from early markets to mainstream markets.

Conclusion

The future of medical tourism industry depends on how well we understand the needs of the medical travelers. The industry is definitely going through a transition from early market adopters to mainstream market. The needs and characteristics of the mainstream market would require us to rethink market strategy and how we will grow, and compete, in the new world of medical tourism.

The mainstream market will compel us to focus on medical tourism products and services that are customer-centric. We have to establish what will set us apart in the crowded marketplace. In this market, it won't be about your value proposition, but we have to think how customer perceives your value proposition.

In order to become market leaders in the mainstream market, you have to know who you are and what you have to offer. Whether you are product innovators, or excel in customer service, or provide the lowest cost solution, you cannot be everything to everyone. By thinking that you can represent yourself in all three categories, you'll blur your messages to your customer and hence be unable to establish your true identity.

The medical tourism sustainability model is based on establishing a solid foundation and infrastructure for an organization to grow. The key pillars of sustainable medical tourism infrastructure are partnership and alliances formed to enhance the overall value proposition of an organization. When coupled with understanding of supply chain and true respect for competitive environment of medical tourism, a winning strategy can be established. The evolution of the industry will definitely will rely on entrepreneurs who have always been leading innovators of disruptive solutions in the world.

In order to develop innovative strategies we need to understand how we will find our potential customers, how we will nurture their relationship, and how we will delight them with our unique, unparalleled quest for highest ethical service results.

Chapter 3: Findability

Introduction

Findability refers to our search for information, based on our specific needs. The term also applies to how easily (or not) we find relevant information most able to deal with our own current situations.

Whether we're looking for generic information or focused and specific information, finding the right solution is based on the concept of one that offers the best options.

Some of the most important key words in this endeavor include accessibility of information, relevancy to our needs, retrieval of information to solve my problems, and discovering ways to solve my problems. If you're looking to attract patients, whether they're local, regional, or global, your approach to information dissemination is vital. How will you offer information to the public so that you find patients targeted to what you're offering?

Ask yourself this: How can your

healthcare products and services be presented to your potential customers when they're in process of discovering ways to solve their problems? It's important at this stage to focus on the customer, and not yourself. Knowing customer needs (not your own) is the key to success in any business. When you perform a 'needs analysis' of a customer, you must understand the when, what, where, how, why, etc., along with their cultural background abehavior.

You must understand what problems people are trying to solve and give them information on how they can go about it. If you focus on your potential customer's behavior, culture, and needs and not what you're trying to sell, you'll be better able to match your products and services than your competition.

In this chapter we will evaluate how to find people who may be interested in your services.

In order to assess your specific target market it is important to understand the supply and demand of the industry. Based on supply demand analysis you will able to understand competitive nature of your business and it will help you define how to create and position your healthcare products and services.

Once we have understood the nature of demand and associated competitive landscape, we will further analyze how to target the audience. This will include understanding Personas. Personas will define how you will meet the needs of the demand and would define an approach to reach out to that market segmentation. We must evaluate and understand our customer's "persona". We'll talk more about how to create a persona of our target audience.

Then we will evaluate the marketing and educational channels we can use to get our message out to the consumers we are targeting. Whether this is online or physical channel through a local doctor, or advertising for our services in TV ads - we must thoroughly understand the impact and cost benefit of that channel. Understanding marketing insights will give us an understanding of *key performance indicators* (KPIs) and how to evaluate each applicable channel to maximize tangible business analytics to establish true ROI (*return on investment*).

Based on these targeted marketing concepts, we will summarize our finding and perhaps develop a blue print to attain and execute overall plan to create a competitive way to find the patients who are in our target market.

Dealing with Supply and Demand in Medical Tourism

Supply and demand is perhaps one of the most fundamental concepts of market economy. Demand represents how much of product or services are desired by the buyers. Quantity is defined as the amount of a product people are willing to buy at a certain price. Supply is defined by how much of a product or service the market can offer. The quantity supplied refers to the amount of a certain good producers are willing to supply when receiving certain price.

Medical Tourism Demand

| Income | Substitute Products | Complementary Services | No. of Buyers | Tastes & Preferences |

Medical services consumers are willing and able to buy at different possible prices

Medical Tourism Supply

| No. of Sellers | Cost of Services | Productivity | Technology | Provider Expectations |

Medical services that are available at all possible prices in the market

Picture 3.1 Medical Service Supply and Demand Model

In the world of healthcare, demand of healthcare services is influenced by price. Generally, if there is a low supply and a high demand, the price of the healthcare services will be high. In contrast, the greater the healthcare supply and lower the demand, the lower the price will be.

In medical tourism industry, it was initially perceived that the American healthcare system would have a huge impact on the market. When perfor ming a proper demand analysis, it was evident that the actual demand vs. perceived demand had a huge chasm. Based on this perceived demand, a barrage amount of solutions emerged in last 5 to 7 years, where everyone was trying to serve the same market. As it turn out the Ame-rican market's demand for medical tourism related services was limited due to economic crisis, and under-education of the right market about availability of the options.

Medical Tourism Demand

It is increasingly important to understand the factors that are critical to propel the demand in the medical tourism industry. When it applies to demand, medical consumers are often willing and able to buy medical services at different prices. The main influencers that drive demand for global medical include:

Income

The income of people is driven by regional economic factors. Some regions are facing economic crisis while others are seeing economic boom. In any situation, it impacts medical tourism industry positively or negatively.

For example, today we see, due to the ramifications of the economic crisis in the Americas, the demand for medical services abroad using discretionary income are currently low due to lower income levels, while with the growth of the Asian economy's middle class offers them access to increased options for reliable and high quality treatment abroad.

Substituting Products

As you know, people are always looking for options. Demand for medical services is often driven by availability of "substitute" services and products.

The "substitute" services in medical tourism world relates to alternatives to current therapies, such as stem cell solutions for chronic diseases or accessibility and availability of procedures not approved in the person's country of origin. Such products and services may include alternative medicines available in other regions/countries.

The emergence of substitute product is also driven by cost. When the cost of a product or services increases beyond means in one area, other cost effective solutions in other countries emerge and brings equilibrium. This is a key factor that propels medical tourism industry where world is becoming a level playing field.

Complementary Services

Demand is generally also propelled by complementary services bundled together making it a more comprehensive solution. In medical tourism industry defining complementary services as part of the overall solution is key to driving demand. Some of the complementary products in the medical tourism industry include airport pick-up/drop-off, hotel arrangements, spa services, among many other services that can be bundled to create a very unique medical tourism product and make customer feel like kings and queens.

Number of Buyers of Healthcare Services

Healthcare services are consumed by every living being. The key is to understand and customize your solutions for the specific buyers of healthcare services. Driving demand from a larger segmentation of the population would mean more consumers will be aware of what is available. Targeted marketing effort based on specific target persona is the key to increase the number of buyers for your healthcare solution.

Tastes and Preferences

Tastes and preferences are the subjective side of consumers' choice. They are driven by trends, fashions, knowledge, friends, education, culture and advertising. As consumers' tastes and preferences changes, so does the demand. It can positively or negatively influences the market. So in order to propel medical tourism demand we have to keep eye on the latest trends and consumer preferences.

Medical Tourism Supply

In the medical tourism industry, supply-side is represented by number of medical providers as well as service facilitators among others. Over last few years, it appears that the medical providers have assumed unlimited capacity in their facilities for international patients, as it provides image, foreign exchange, among other benefits. The supply side is influenced by following factors:

Number of Sellers

Number of sellers in the market place determines how competitive the environment is. More sellers of like products mean high supply. Medical tourism industry could have over 40,000+ medical service providers competing in local, regional and global levels. This high number of provider base has created excess supply of product in the marketplace.

Cost of Service

When the supply of any products and services increases, the price decreases. In medical tourism industry, as the supply continues to grow with un-proportionate increase in demand, the industry is facing price war challenges with limited product differentiators.

Productivity

Productivity is a key element of supply. When productivity is high, it can change the price point. In medical tourism industry the supply is impacted when there is an increase productivity as more patients can be treated with same infrastructure and hence increasing the margins.

Technology

Supply is also influenced by introduction and utilization of technology. In medical tourism industry with availability of same medical equipment around the world as well as other industry technological innovations becoming common practice, it has impact on greater patient flow, rate of successful treatments, among the others. Technology can also have an impact on supply curve.

Finding Your Equilibrium

Balancing supply and demand is not always easy. The term *'equilibrium'* defines the process of providing quality and price with the quantity of services or options that intersect your supply and demand curves. For example, when costs and options are offered that meet customer demand and expectations.

In order to affect the demand for medical tourism and bring equilibrium between supply and demand – some of the following initiatives will help:

- Cost and cost changes
- Consumer disposal income
- Changing consumer perception and preferences
- Product substitutes and complementary product packaging
- Government policies
- Technological innovations
- Marketing and advertising to targeted audience
- Sociological demographic marketing

In medical tourism industry, we currently have imbalance between supply and demand. We need to proper the demand to meet the available supply for this industry to grow. Obtaining equilibrium in the equation is essential for industry to sustain and flourish. To bring equilibrium in the supply and demand, we must understand the personas of medical traveler's needs. In order to propel demand by developing products and services that will form equilibrium between supply and demand in the medical tourism industry we must understand our customers and their respective needs, and personas.

Healthcare Customer Behavior: New Healthcare Consumers

Buying Behavior in a Global Marketplace

We've seen a change in the way consumers approach healthcare. They're more knowledgeable and willing to take charge of their healthcare decisions. Take a look at the list of common factors that drive healthcare decisions today:

• Control: Customers choose when and how they engage
• Expectations: Customers need complete information & case histories
• Choices: Customers have limitless choices
• Global Solution: Customers can buy from anywhere in the world
• Peer Reviews

Just like anything these days, the internet offers consumers the option to shop for products and services globally. Likewise, the healthcare industry is also controlled by an increase in consumer choices. Whether it is local or international, consumers are engaged in market research regarding medical conditions and treatment options, thanks to such connectivity. They're taking control of their medical and healthcare options.

Consumers are making decisions regarding medical providers for the treatment of specific conditions. They don't necessarily want the same doctor to solve all their problems; they're looking for specialists to treat specific conditions.

Before deciding on their medical providers, consumers need, and expect, information at their fingertips. Such information includes a doctor's educational background, patient stories, case studies, etc.

How do they do this? Check it out.

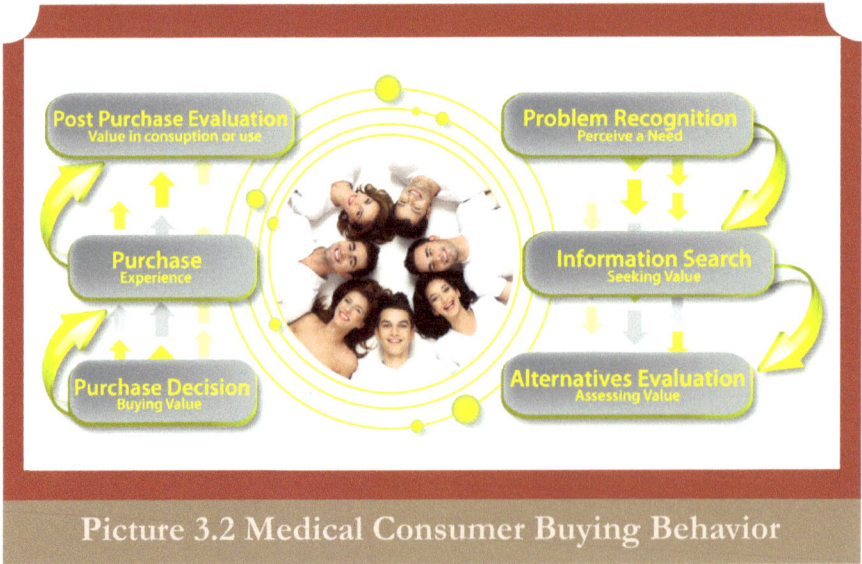

Picture 3.2 Medical Consumer Buying Behavior

Personas: Do You Know Who Your Customers Are?

Do you really know your target customers? Can you clearly define their characteristics in terms of who are they, where they live, their motivations, what information they need before they buy, their economic conditions, or why they would want your services?

One of the most important things you can do to help make your service more relevant is to get to know your customers. Conducting analysis, soliciting patient feedback, interviewing and surveying are all good ways of doing this, but there are many more. You can further increase the usefulness of this information, as well as add to it, by creating personas for your customers.

Personas are an extremely valuable tool for defining customer profiles in any field. If you're not familiar with the term, here's a brief definition:

Personas are representations of your target audience that you're trying to attract to your clinic or hospital based on demographics and socio-economic conditions.

A **persona** is a customer profile that you can use to help make consumption decisions. These profiles are created from knowledge usually gained from current patient bases and research. Think of a **persona model** as having a "virtual" customer to bounce ideas off of and help you keep the goals of the customer in mind on a day-to-day basis.

From individual doctors to clinics to hospitals, anyone can benefit from developing personas of their prospective patients and their own brand to gain competitive advantages.

What are Personas and Why Do We Need Them?

A **persona** typically involves giving a fictitious name and characteristics to a 'client' that is consistent with one of the main consumer groups you have identified for the services you are offering.

Personas put a face on the customer. Some persona programs give people names so you can refer to them and see them in a "physical" manifestation or representation. A persona removes the tendency to think of yourself as the customer, and instead forces you to step back and visualize your customers. This method offers the structure to do so.

Some of the key elements of **persona** development include:

1. Who are your customers?
2. Why are they looking for services?
3. What is important to them?
4. What do they need to know?
5. Where will they look?
6. How do they decide?

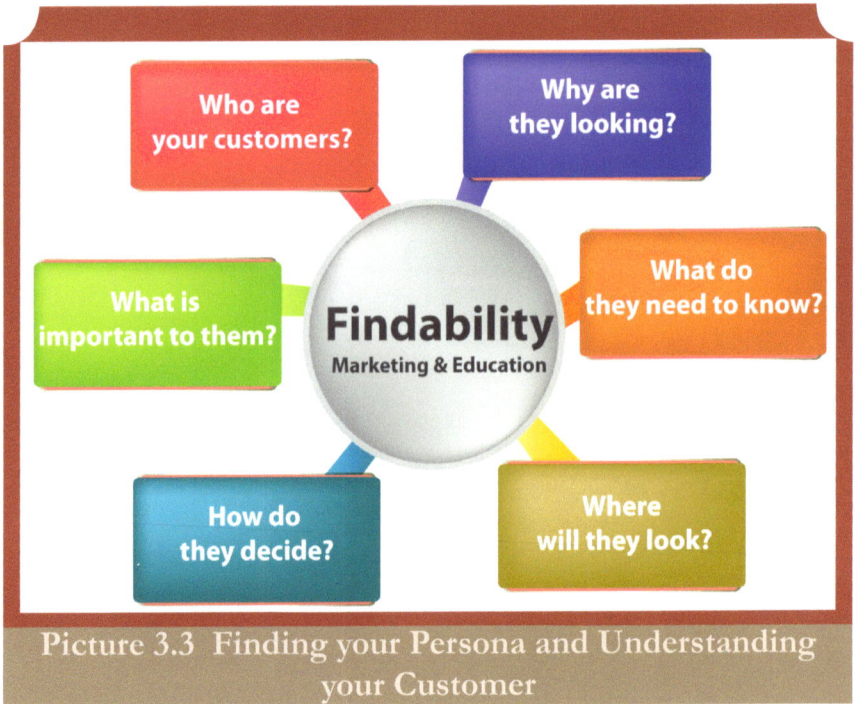

Picture 3.3 Finding your Persona and Understanding your Customer

What are some characteristics of Personas that need to be defined?

- Persona name
- Demographics: age group, gender, education, ethnicity, family status, location
- Type of Profession: job title and major responsibilities in professional life
- Decision Maker or Head of Household?
- Economics – yearly income, type of home, home value
- Goals and tasks in relation to your services
- Environment – physical, social, technological

What are the Key Questions a Persona should address?

- Why would this person be interested in your products and services?
- What questions or concerns does this person have about your products and services?
- What key information do we want to communicate to this person?
- What challenges do we face in achieving our communication goals?
- What are this person's media habits?
- What challenges does this person face at work/home?
- Describe this person's decision-making process?
- Where does this person shop?
- A quote that sums up what matters most to the persona with relevance for your services.

How do you Develop Personas?

The first and most important thing you'll need to do before developing a persona is to gather information about your patients. How you do this depends on your resources and budget. We'll offer a few simple tips to help you create your personas.

The best personas will also go the extra step by describing key behaviors such as the decision-making process, information-browsing approaches, or shopping modes and habits—the drivers that affect how people approach a given solution.

Ask these questions:

1. *Finding patients* - Who are the prospective patients? How many are there? What do they do with the services/brand that you are offering?
2. *Building a hypothesis* - What are the differences (cultural, beliefs, attitudes) between patients from different backgrounds?
3. *Verifications*: Compile data for personas (likes/dislikes, inner needs, values), data for situations (area of work, work conditions), data for scenarios (work and information strategies and goals).

4. *Finding patterns:* Does the initial labeling hold? Are there more groups to consider? Are all equally important?
5. *Constructing personas:* Body (name, age picture). Psyche (extrovert/introvert). Background (occupation). Emotions and attitude toward seeking alternative healthcare options, the company (sender) or the information that they need. Don't forget personal traits.
6. *Defining situations* - What is the need of this persona?   7   .
7. *Validation and buy-in* - Do you know someone like this?
8. *Dissemination of knowledge:* How can we share the personas with the organization?
9. *Creating scenarios* - In a given situation, with a given goal, what happens when the persona engages with the brand?
10. *On-going development* - Does new information alter the personas?

Examples

Elective Procedure Medical Tourist

Our primary persona seeking elective procedures such as cosmetic surgery is "Jenny" who is between 40-45 years old. She values her appearance and has some disposal income. Jenny leads an active life and would consider going abroad to save some money for improving her appearance. You would find an image of her to use in your planning, a visual reminder of her type. Before deciding on type and place for the surgery, she will perform serious research. She has high need for information, e.g., who will perform the surgery, do they carry relevant board certification, are there good sight-seeing or relaxing opportunities before and after the procedure, good restaurants, shopping opportunities, etc.

Jenny will shop around for the procedure to determine which provider and location will provide the best value for her hard earned money. She will most likely need a broad scope and depth of information and use a guide more intensely. In fact, she would probably prefer a pre packaged product to meet her needs.

As you start making decisions about service and marketing strategies, you would check back to "Jenny" and ask yourself if such decisions would affect her or her needs. If not, what would reach her more effectively? What message does she need to hear?

Surgical Procedure Medical Tourist

Our persona for surgical procedure is "Steve" who is 60-65 years of age, is on fixed income, and has been considering a hip replacement surgery. He has no insurance and would not be able to afford such surgery locally. His activities have been limited over the years due to hip problems and he has a strong desire to play with his grand kids. He has traveled internationally before and would consider going abroad for his hip surgery. He would perform an in-depth research on the hospital and surgeon who will perform surgery on him, the type of materials they will use, and sanitary conditions, among other key factors.

Steve is very sensitive about the end results and would like to see a doctor and hospital's track record of performing similar surgeries. He won't consider the sight- seeing or tourism aspect as the primary reason for medical travel. He will be very time-conscious and would focus on his surgery and recovery period. He would be a value traveler and most likely to put his own trip together after careful consideration of doctor, hospital, location, flight, etc.

Complementary and Alternative Medicine Medical Tourist

Our persona seeking integrative or alternative treatment is "Pam". Pam is 35-40 years old, educated and has a higher household income. She has strong beliefs in organic and holistic products and services. She is very health-conscious and would like to do the same for all her family members. She will always search for alternative ways to treat any symptoms for her family.

She would indulge herself going to the source or origin of particular alternative medicine in a foreign country to learn and obtain the best treatment from the "experts".

Generally, money is not a huge concern; the main focus is authenticity. Pam considers herself a trend follower. She is a leisure traveler and a tourist when she travels abroad for alternative or integrated medicine treatment. She would enjoy packaged products and services that include everything required for her treatment and hence making the decision making process very simple and easy.

Using appropriate personas e.g., you can determine the behavior of a patient. For example, when responding to an email inquiry from a patient, ask yourself, "When Jenny, Steve or Pam receive this email, how would they react?" Would THEY be satisfied with the information provided in the email? Would THEY jump on a plane and come to your facility for treatment OR what more do they need to know before they made up their mind?

Hence, putting yourself in the patient's shoes will help you understand the situation better and hopefully your response to a patient inquiry will be more personal. Your chances of closing the deal with the patient would be much higher.

Always ask:

• "How would my persona react when they receive this email from me?" or "Will my persona from America will come to my facility considering the current economic crisis in America?"
• Will my persona has the money to travel to my center for an elective procedure or will he or she wait?" Answering such questions will help you define new ways to attract people from new locations by fine-tuning your services and becoming innovative.

Benefits of Creating a Persona Model

• Better understanding of your customers.
• Improved product and service quality.

- Targeted consumer goals. Needs become a common focal point for your services
- By always asking, "Would my persona use this?" the team can avoid the trap of building what consumer asks for rather than what they will actually use.
- Services can be prioritized based on the personas.
- Disagreements over service and pricing decisions can be sorted out by referring back to the personas.
- Services can be constantly evaluated against the personas, generating better services.

You'll want to develop several personas - perhaps seven or eight initially for the clinic, to ensure that you explore all the needs of your user base. The simplicity of the end product—a rich description of a person who represents a like group of customers—can make persona creation seem easy.

Do fun exercises in your office and create a persona of your typical customer – try to answer all the questions listed in this white paper to determine if you see a trend among a set group of clients you tend to attract. We would love it if you shared your results with us.

Know your customers!
Use personas when defining your products and services and turn your business into a sales machine!

Major Marketing Channels

In order to service the market, to increase the awareness and hence the demand, and based on target personas, the key marketing channels needs to be established. These marketing channels need to be carefully evaluated and identify which of these channels will have the greatest impact for your products and services.

Based on our extensive research, following are some of the findings in the medical tourism marketing channels to find right targeted customers:

Channels	Cost	Cost Per Acquisition	Exposure / Impressions	Lead Time	Flexibility	Scalability	Sustainable
Online	Low	Low	High	Low	High	High	Yes
Insurance	Medium	Medium	Medium	High	Low	Medium	Yes
Medical Provider Referral	Medium	Low	Medium	Medium	Low	Low	Yes
Print Media	High	High	Medium	Medium	Low	Low	No
TV/Radio	High	High	High	Medium	Low	Low	No
Word of Mouth	Low	Low	Low	High	Low	Low	No

Picture 3.4 Medical Tourism Marketing Channels

What are some key observations you can make by analyzing the marketing channels in the marketplace? Which channel is more suitable to your organizational situation?

When attempting to focus on the most important component of a medical marketing program, we identified the following metric (or key measurements for analysis):

Cost and Cost per Acquisition – What is your total affordable budget for marketing initiatives? How much it costs to acquire an international patient?

How much are you willing to pay in marketing expenses to create a sustainable business?

Exposure – How much market presence you will get from this marketing approach? How many people will see your brand from this marketing channel?

Lead time – How long it will take for a marketing channel to produce results i.e., international patients? Do you have business flexibility to sustain the program for a long-term?

Flexibility and Scalability – does the marketing method allow you to adjust and sharpen your message as you learn more about your target market, or is it rigid? Can you expand your marketing reach easily and quickly through this marketing channel?

Based on this data, we reviewed and analyzed overall which marketing channels are sustainable and most suitable for medical tourism programs. The sustainability of the channel was considered over a 3 to 5 year period and not as a short-term solution.

Based on these criterion and detailed analytical evaluation of the industry parameters – three main marketing channels emerged that presents most promising results:

Online Marketing – online marketing provides a continuously rapidly growing marketing platform which is affordable, customizable, and can produce results fairly quickly. It is also deemed easily scalable while being completely flexible to introduce new products, services, or conceptual ideas into the market.

Medical Provider Referrals – medical provider referral channel is another key component of the supply chain, which has been a traditional way of referring patients between a generalist to specialist. If designed and executed properly, this could also be a sustainable marketing program when combined with pre-and post-care as well as value added services.

Insurance or group associations – third party payers or associations which can influence a buying decision of a market segment is a critical element of the value chain in medical tourism. Understanding and educating this segment and establish a win-win value proposition is essential in growing the real demand for a long sustainable patient acquisition.

You would need to evaluate your business environment, customer personas, and your own products and services to determine which marketing channel you would like to invest in. As each marketing channel is quite different from each other, the value chain among all must be clearly understood and financial decisions should be made accordingly. The key to maximize your results based on tangible parameters.

Medical Tourism and Online Marketing

As discussed earlier, web is one of the most critical marketing channel to educate your targeted market segment about your products and services. Of all media, it is the only place consumers can fully experience your health services without physically visiting your facility. You must create an emotional and intellectual experience that will stimulate the same response from the users as when they visit your facility for real.

Targeted
Selected Audience
Customizable Message

Affordable
Lower Cost of Acquisition
Customizable Budget

Global
Worldwide Audience
Multiple Languages

Picture 3.5 Medical Tourism Online Marketing Channel

Share | Interact | Connect | Engage

Share

In medical tourism industry, it is very critical that you are able to share your credentials with your target audience remotely. As the buying decision starts with identifying the problem and searching for respective solution, it is essential that you educate your audience by sharing your offering not from sales point of view but educational material point of view.

Interact

Web presence gives you an opportunity to interact proactively with your targeted consumer. You can now develop targeted communities to interact with the consumer and educate them. Interactivity is key to influence the healthcare buyer about your programs and also be influenced by their needs. It is a part of communication that is a critical component of new healthcare consumer buying behavior.

Connect

When you share and interact with the healthcare consumer, you will be able to connect with them in a meaning way. Social connection is important to build a long lasting customer relationship, which will not only help with addressing current customer needs but also with their friends and family in the future.

Engage

For your brand to have lasting impact on the targeted consumer base, your brand should represent authenticity which will come after you fully engage in solving customer's problems. Honest, open, humble communication with the customer will draw them towards your solution and keeping them engage not only during the product-buying cycle, but also post-buying experience will draw a longer term benefit.

Targeted Market Segmentation

Segmenting the specific market to present your products and services will produce more tangible results and reduce the overall cost of marketing. A well-defined target market is the key element to a marketing strategy.

Target market segmentation is grouping of audience in categories that are distinguishable and noticeable. The variables to consider when targeting your customers in medical tourism industry are:

1. *Treatments*: Medical conditions the products and services Addresses
2. *Geographic*: Geographical locations including proximity of customer base
3. *Demographics*: socioeconomics by gender, age, income, occupation, education, etc.

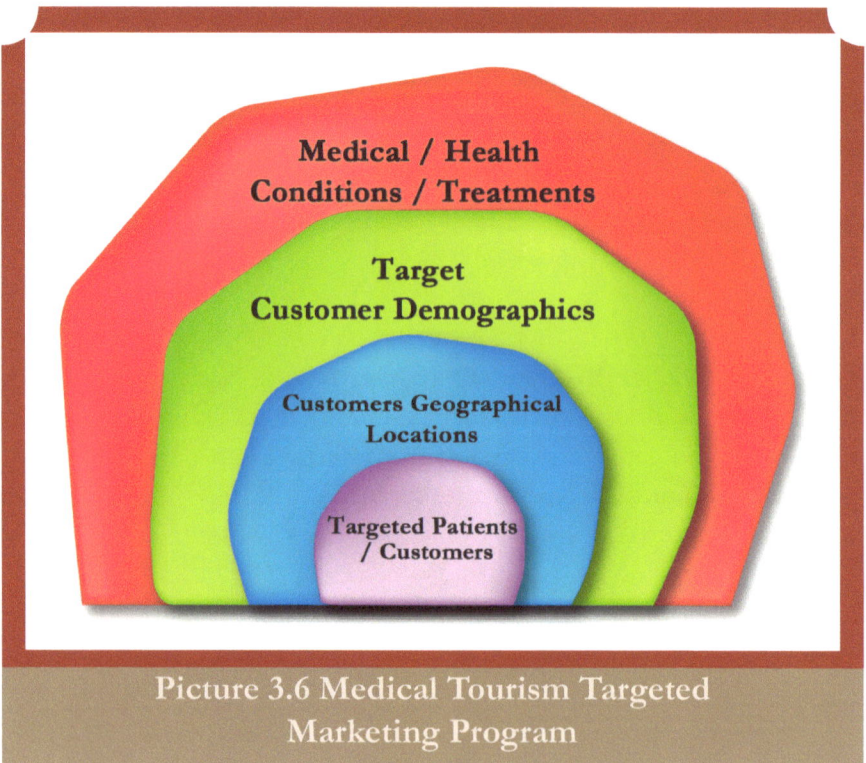

Medical / Health Conditions / Treatments

Target Customer Demographics

Customers Geographical Locations

Targeted Patients / Customers

Picture 3.6 Medical Tourism Targeted Marketing Program

Condition / Treatment Based Market Segmentation

It is critical to segment the market based on specific health problems people are trying to solve. For example, people who have bad knee will look for knee specific information and solutions. The condition-based marketing relates to causes of the problem, symptoms, condition, and available treatments or options to address the issue at hand.

In medical tourism, people are looking for all types of conditions from beauty to chronic diseases, to preventive medicine, and to life threatening diseases such as cancer, heart surgery, etc.

Behavior and Demographic Targeting

Identifying a targeted audience that would appeal to your product is the key. Behavioral targeting is increasingly becoming critical, and allows marketers to understand healthcare consumers and their buying behaviors and patterns. Only then can they (the provider) relay engaging messages based on these search patterns.

Demographics-based targeting means understanding medical tourism market, aligned with products. For example, cosmetic surgery may be more appealing to females ranging between 35 to 50 years with disposal income, while critical surgeries such as hip replacement may be more applicable for baby boomers. The determining variables to understand your demographics include: gender, age, income, education, ethnicity, and language, among others.

Geo Targeting Based Marketing

Geo targeting is extremely critical to understand your real customer base in medical tourism industry. The more we learn about the patterns associa ted with where the customers are coming from and design healthcare products and services for that market will result in higher patients and overall success.

The geo-targeting will help you define your whether your market is local, regional or global. In the medical tourism industry, we are observing the trends are based on distance, flight connectivity, travel time, and overall trends and consumer experience from that region.

Increasingly in medical tourism industry, general "catch-all" messaging is no longer effective. We have to deliver a specific message targeted for a specific treatment, for a specific demographics, based on a specific location. These messages and marketing campaigns should be customized for each segmentation based on defined criteria for that market. This is the only way we can differentiate the medical tourism products and services in the highly competitive marketplace.

Medical Tourism Marketing Return on Investment (ROI) Analysis

"You cannot manage something you cannot control, and you cannot control something you cannot measure." - Peter Drucker

So far in medical tourism industry, very few organizations have embraced how to measure the results. It is very critical for us to collect the right data and establish key performance indicators (KPIs) to measure the performance. Marketing initiatives whether online or insurance or other referrals should be measured to determine what the return on investment would be. A simple methodology to measure the returns is:

Key Performance Indicators Methodology

1. Decide what measures to take and then make sure those measures meet your needs
2. Collect Data - ensure you have robust systems and clear roles and responsibilities
3. Calculate Performance - use standard approaches where possible
4. Report Results - communicate quickly to all stakeholders
5. Analyze Results - ask questions - what is the data telling you
6. Take Action - this is where the value is generated!
7. Measure Again… for continuous improvement

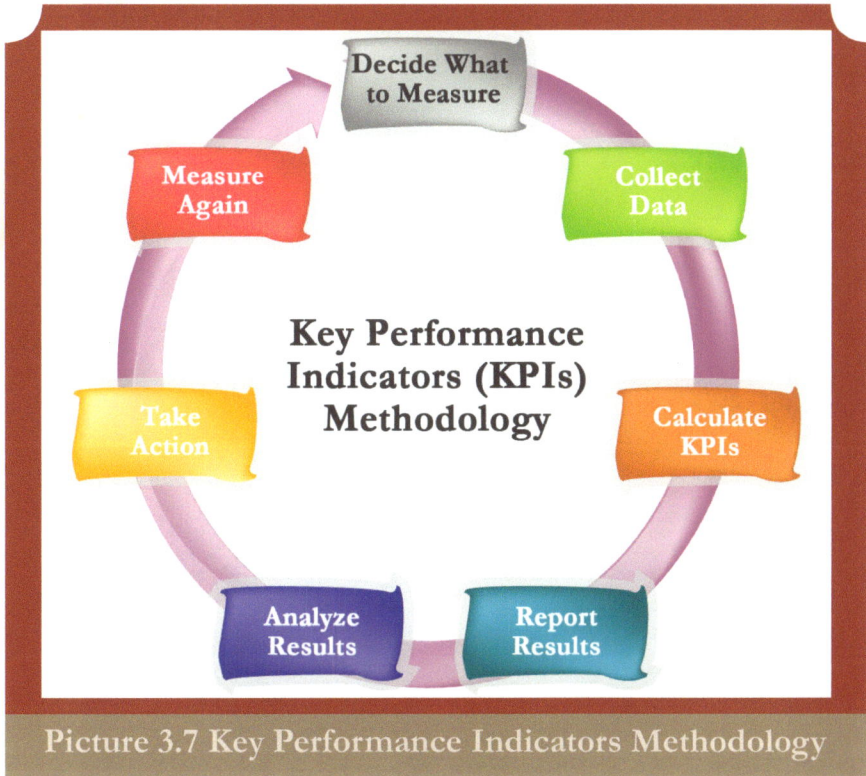

Picture 3.7 Key Performance Indicators Methodology

Key Performance Indicators (KPIs) for Online Marketing

The key performance indicators (KPIs) are commonly used by organizations to measure the performance of a particular activity. The performance is measured against defined goals and objectives established by the organization in order to run a successful business. It helps understand how well we are performing in relations to what we want to achieve and whether we are on track with them.

KPIs help to understand complex organizational performance into a small number of key indicators that help understand the progress. As in medical business when we go to a doctor, the first thing the doctor's office does is to take measurements such as blood pressure, cholesterol levels, weight, height to determine a baseline of your health condition. Once they start treating you, the progress is measured against same parameters to see if improvements are occurring against defined goals.

Similarly, in medical tourism industry it is essential to see measure the progress against tangible and sensible measurable goals.

In medical tourism marketing we can establish non-financial as well as financial KPIs to measure the effectiveness of a marketing channel. It is extremely important to measure your efforts in marketing by:

Non-Financial KPIs

- Unique Visitors | Organic Traffic
- Ad Impressions
- Page Ranks | Pages Indexed
- Click Through
- Tweeter Followers | Facebook Friends
- Blog Comments
- Video Views | PR Views
- Delivered Emails

Financial KPIs

- No. of Patients Leads
- Cost Per Acquisition of Patient Leads
- % of Leads Converted into Patients
- Revenues from Converted Patients
- ROI = (Revenues - Investment) / Investment

Picture 3.8 Financial and Non-Financial Key Performance Indicators

Non- Financial KPIs

Non-financial indicators measure overall health of a marketing campaign and determine whether set of variables are resulting in tangible progress overtime. For example, is there a positive movement in number of visitors to a site, number of comments, number of likes, number of followers, number of open emails, etc. These KPIs are essential to manage overall performance of an online campaign.

Financial KPIs

Financial KPIs are tangible outcome of a campaign which results in a financial benefit to an organization. Parameters such as marketing cost, market cost per patient, return on investments are critical to measure as they will determine whether we need to continue to investing in that campaign or take other initiatives.

Findability
Medical Tourism Marketing and Education

Findability is the key to understand your consumer base. We need to understand what drives consumer demand. Once we have understood the nature of demand and associated competitive supply landscapes, we can establish which audience we need to target. Developing personas to understand your targeted consumer base will help define the main market characteristics and the specific marketing message and method for which this segment is ready.

Based on your specific targeted persona, an evaluation of educational and marketing channel will establish a message and communication distribution strategy. Whether we use online marketing or physical channels through a local doctor referral program or advertising for your services on TV ads, you must thoroughly understand overall sustainable economic and financial impacts. Understanding the marketing channels as associated cost benefit will give us an understanding of key performance indicators (KPIs) and how to maximize tangible business analytics to establish true ROI (return on investment).

Based on these targeted marketing concepts, we can establish best way to **FIND** our right customer who will maximize the results for our medical tourism program. Shooting in the dark, developing "catch all" strategy will not result in sustainable success, but will drain financial resources and hence exit of an organization from the medical tourism market.

Remember, in order to find our target market, we must find our customers. We must analyze culture, behavior, trend, and most specifically their needs. Customer needs analysis will drive the next generation of the competitive marketplace.

Balancing supply and demand is not always easy. The term 'equilibrium' defines the process of providing quality and price with the quantity of services or options that intersect your supply and demand curves. For example, when costs and options are offered that meet customer demand and expectations.

Remember to define the persona of your targeted customer market. Only by doing so will you succeed. Now, it's time to move on to the topic of sellability. What is sellability? It's more than the ability to sell products or services to your customers. It involves brand recognition, value perception and your ability to customize services to best meet the needs of your customers.

Chapter 4: Sellability: Nurturing and Convincing

Introduction

Sellability is defined as an ability to sell a solution to a prospective customer. Today's healthcare consumers are connected, impatient, self-sufficient, elusive, impulsive, and highly informed, and that's just the tip of the iceberg.

This abundance of information makes it ever more difficult for you to promote your services to customers, and often elicits a defensive reaction among providers in the reaction to and competing on price.

This new breed of informed buyers and consumers has caused more than one industry to rethink their strategies and positions regarding sales process and methodologies. So ask yourself this... can you adapt to this new consumer buying behavior and make necessary changes in your approach?

If your answer is "no," you'd better get out of the medical tourism business.

Important questions to ask yourself about Sellability are:

1. Is your brand recognizable beyond local boundaries?
2. Do you customize your services for your customers?
3. What is your unique value proposition?
4. Are you dealing with a price war? How to deal with it?

Nurturing customer leads which generate patients that benefit your business's top line revenue requires a multitude of methods, the most important of which is communication. However, communication itself needs to nurture trust, compassion, understanding, as well as inspire, encourage, and inform our prospective customers.

In this chapter, we will discuss some of the ways you can position yourself effectively, by understanding the buying behavior of your customers. We will walk through a systematic process of understanding consumers' needs, establishing human touch to the process while understanding how to negotiate with this smart consumer to meet their needs and desires while winning them over. We will also discuss how to establish a selling value proposition to avoid current price war game in the medical tourism industry. The chapter will tie these themes together to generate a guideline to win the customer for your business!

Patient Nurturing and Selling

Once you acquire a patient lead through effective marketing and educational approaches, you must nurture that lead. You must work hard to convince the patient that you are the best solution for him or her. Some healthcare providers mistakenly believe this aspect of healthcare doesn't rest on their shoulders.

On the contrary, the best "salesperson" in an organization is the organization/provider itself. In order to generate and maintain total customer satisfaction and quality, you, the healthcare provider, must able to control this process effectively. You must be able to offer any patient the best experience of their life.

The Importance of the Human Experience

The healthcare providers constantly deal with extreme human emotions. For that reason it is critical to nurture compassion and empathy and offer patients the expertise, information and results they're looking for in the most effective manner possible. The result of this phase is a patient that has ultimately decided to explore your services and visit your facilities.

Major factors involved in this process from the patient's perspective include:

• Language – can you speak in a language that patient can understand? Communications is the key to any effective healthcare service.
• How do you amass information about a patient's condition?
• What do you offer regarding treatment plans? How are you unique?
• How well do you answer questions about the importance of their specific treatment?
• Do you offer evaluation specialists when necessary during the nurturing process?
• Do you offer multiple treatment options and choices when possible?
• Do you provide travel and accommodation considerations

Positioning Yourself Effectively

In the medical field, and specifically medical travel, the ability to position and sell value effectively is critical, more now than ever before. Consumers are socially connected and fluid in their thinking and ideas, depending on situation.

Medical providers and/or government health agencies who are able to adapt to this new understanding from consumers, and analyze their wants and needs, will be the ones to succeed in the next generation of medical tourism business.

This new generation of medical travelers has evolved through today's wide access to social media and literally tons of information. They're less reliant on a specific medical provider's perceived diagnosis and solutions. These informed individuals are often able to identify their own conditions, conduct research independently, access peer and professional knowledge, and ask questions, receive answers and participate in related blogs and forums. They're able to define what they're looking for when evaluating their selection of a healthcare provider or facility to meet their needs.

Adapting to this new paradigm requires a new way of thinking; a new framework, skills, activities, and tools that are now essential for effective patient acquisition. You need to be willing to adapt your execution strategy and explore how your processes, methodologies, and specific skills and needs can be adapted to this new breed of customer or buyer.

What is this New Aspect of "Sellability" in Medical Travel?

What does this new approach demand from you, the medical provider? Check it out:

- **Process** – Defining your international patient coordination process will not only help with what to do, but also it will establish how things should be done.
- **Philosophy** - The customer must be the focus. Your first goal is to help your customers solve their health problems. Give them the best solutions to help them reach positive and measurable results or outcomes to their problems.
- **Guide** - Your ability to guide your customer from where they are now to where they want to be in the future – a map of their present condition to future desired state.
- **Methodology** - You must be able to provide methods that include tools, techniques, and procedures - a complete system that helps your customer achieve their goals.
- **Customer Management System** - Effectively manage and analyze your processes and pipelines in order to help manage your customers and their expectations.

Sellability…
Means Understanding Your Customer Needs

Take a look at the graphic… what do you see? You see points that every customer wants when it comes to their healthcare services and products. Learn them… memorize them. They're the foundation of your ability to provide quality, customer-based services to your clients, now and in the future.

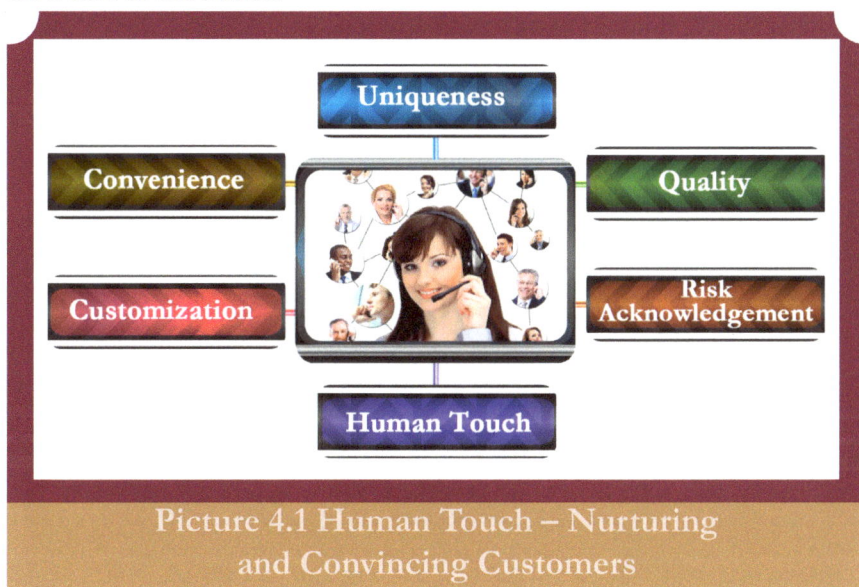

Picture 4.1 Human Touch – Nurturing and Convincing Customers

Let's take a moment to talk about the human touch concept. What does it mean? What does it sound like? The human touch personifies the services you offer your clients, though human contact. It involves:

- **Convenience** – readily accessible information: services, price, unique selling proposition, assurance & safety
- **Customization** – customized treatment plans for each customer
- **Risk Acknowledgement** - honesty and transparency - techniques, risks, benefits of any treatment
- **Uniqueness** – leadership, customer service, cost/price
- **Quality** – total customer experience reflects quality

Key Factors that Convince a Patient to come to your Facility

Are you providing the best services for your clients? Medical care providers need to be aware that consumers are looking for specific answers when they shop for anything, and that goes from a new car to clothes to medical services.

Medical tourism industry is growing on a daily basis, and becoming highly competitive. In order to develop confidence and trust healthcare service providers should be aware of six very important areas to be addressed. These areas include:

Convenience

Today's consumers literally have the world at their fingertips. Internet access has increased the ability of consumers to compare, explore, and access huge databases searching for a wide range of services and products. When it comes to health care, providers need to focus on a client's ability to access a wide range of information for their needs. For providing medical services abroad, you must able to clearly and easily able to provide following information to the consumers proactively:

- **Pricing**
- **Assurance & safety**
- **Accommodations**
- **Recovery support services**
- **Accessibility**

Whether through the Internet or the printed word, consumers prefer to have such questions answered easily and without being required to spend time researching themselves or pushing hard to obtain some basic understanding of the treatment options. Providing user-friendly access and information that will satisfy the initial curiosity of a consumer is essential for increasing your client base.

You have to make health-buying service processes convenient and easy for consumers. Mainstream customers do not want to spend time and energy in complex processes where they have to "translate" what you intend to say, whether due to language differences or technical medical terminology. The entire buying experience should be seamless and fully integrated and presented as easy step 1, 2, 3. Learn from the experience of successful products in the world. When buying processes are complex, involve too many steps, too many people, too many forms, or too complex medical jargon, people walk away from it and move toward a simpler solution. Customer convenience is critical to a successful program.

Customized Services

Customizing services is also very important in any medical tourism field. Healthcare providers who are able to offer a variety of medical services, surgical techniques and treatments that are customizable according to every patient's individual needs will help to soothe worries and concerns. Customers are increasingly looking for personalized healthcare solutions, so if you can reassure customers that you are capable, willing, and trained to provide services or treatments on a one-on-one basis, your chances of success increase exponentially.

Customization of your services to meet specific patient needs also reinforces your reputation as a customer-oriented practice. The medical tourism industry can benefit from "mass customization" concepts where 80% of the solutions are designed for a market segmentation using industry standards and best practices and 20% is customized specific to customer's medical needs. The move of medical tourism industry providers toward mass customization of services will establish market leaders.

Risk Acknowledgement and Transparency

Consumers today want to be informed. In the past, people were hesitant to question physicians or surgeons about illnesses, treatment options, surgeries, recovery periods and the risks involved in any aspect of their healthcare.

Transparency is essential for today's patients. The ability of a physician or practice to be open and up-front about techniques, risks, as well as benefits to any treatment or procedure is often the difference between a client choosing your services and those offered by someone else. Everyone appreciates honesty and transparency. Providing honest answers to any questions asked by a client will help to insure them they are your top priority.

The mainstream market will demand more transparency from everyone involved in the supply chain. Healthcare consumers in this new market will follow the trends of travel industry, which demand complete transparency in terms of pricing, treatment outcomes, credentials, certifications, peer customer reviews, and experiences, among many other factors that will propel the industry to a new level.

Uniqueness

Health-care providers and professionals who are able to provide unique solutions for a wide range of scenarios will prove more successful. For example, a client searching for information on a bariatric surgical procedure in South America may be concerned about travel details, arrangements, finding adequate room and board, in addition to undergoing the surgical procedure itself.

Healthcare providers who are able to relieve such concerns by offering specific travel packages, pre-and post-surgical care and accommodations for family members help reduce the anxiety a patient may experience when traveling outside of their home country.

Take the difference between hip resurfacing and hip replacement procedures. Do you offer enough information for your potential clients to understand the difference between the two procedures? Such information should also include expectations, differences, risks and benefits, recovery periods and support for the client's emotional and physical well-being both pre-surgery and post-surgery. This may include consultations and follow-up visits and interviews.

With everyone in the medical tourism industry stating they have the best product, best price, best quality, and best location, there is hardly any difference. You have to define your unique value proposition to differentiate yourself in this crowded market.

Enhancing your Brand Awareness

Any professional, and especially those in the medical field, know that reputation is a vital part of any practice. Without a positive reputation, both within the local community and outlying areas, even the best surgeons or physicians will find themselves struggling.

When it comes to medical tourism, reputation and branding are essential. Have you done all you can to increase awareness of your business or practice to the public at large? Advertising, web presence, technical publications, educational materials for general public, and ample opportunities for contact and customer service all serve to help increase global market branding and reputation.

Quality

One of the most important aspects of any product or service is quality. Take a good look at the quality of services that you and your staff or facility provides to your customers. Do you keep up to date with the latest developments, techniques and equipment? Do you and your staff members treat every client with courtesy and respect and ensure that every client is offered the best in services, from care before surgery to recovery services and support offered post-surgery? What are your past customers are saying about your quality of service?

Medical tourism is steadily increasing in numbers as well as popularity. To ensure the success of any health tourism business, providers must attract clients who come from a multitude of different countries, languages and cultures and socio-economic backgrounds. Approaching each client as a unique individual and increasing two-way communication between client and provider is one of the most positive aspects of growing any medical practice, whether it's found in New York City or Singapore.

Add the Human Touch to Your Health Care Services

In this day and age, it's easy to take advantage of e-mails and other forms of virtual communication, but don't forget the challenges the healthcare industry faces as it heads into the 21st century - the missing element of the *human touch*.

Medical tourism as an industry is rapidly growing and becoming increasingly competitive. At present, there is more supply of service providers than those demanding healthcare services in many locations around the world. The growing need for affordable healthcare has increased the number of options, treatments and procedures offered in many countries. So you are not only competing locally, you are competing for healthcare seekers regionally and globally. The challenges facing healthcare providers in coming years will be how to best attract customers and clients to *your* specific healthcare services.

Getting Past the Basics

If you're relying on e-mails and traditional mail to contact your customers, you're missing a vital element to communications. Physicians, surgeons, clinics and hospitals need to be able to connect with patients and assure them that their problems will be addressed by your healthcare facilities. Ask yourself these questions regarding your current business methods:

• Who owns your customer relationship – you or someone else?

• How do you nurture customer relationships - from the time you are first contacted by the customer until they come to your facility?

• What actions do you take to create confidence and trust with the customer prior to them making an appointment?

If the answer to these questions is not clearly defined, then you're failing to take advantage of one of the most proactive and productive approaches to enhance, grow your business, and convert customers into paying patients.

The key to such conversion relies on human expressions of compassion, confidence, and trust.

Without communicating in *detail* with prospective patients, it's nearly impossible to understand their specific needs or to create a treatment plan customized to their specific situation. The way to do that is through human contact – the voice.

The Six-Touch Point System

The six-touch point system is an effective method of enhancing communication and to convert potential customers to confirmed patients. The six-touch point system employs the following approach to customer relations:

1.) Introductory e-mails
2.) Customer follow-up call – (the human touch)
3.) Offer customers a detailed treatment plan – how, what, when, who
4.) Offer testimonials and case story successes – past experiences
5.) Customer follow-up call – (the human touch again)
6.) E-mail follow-up and confirmation

Utilizing such an approach, we can ensure that multiple forms of communication are used to create a well-rounded approach to satisfying customer issues, increasing customer acquisition and converting 'possibles' into confirmed clients.

Facing Future Challenges

Advancements in medical technology, tools and equipment has made it easy for healthcare providers to forget the human element in healthcare. However, you can have the most advanced medical or surgical equipment at your disposal, but if you forget to connect to the patient's spiritual, emotional, or mental needs, you may never get a chance to use it.

Healthcare providers must continue to work nurturing and building trusting relationships with prospective patients and help them to understand what they're facing, what their options are, and help them make decisions.

Ask yourself these questions:

• How much time do you spend with patients to listen to their issues, fears, or concerns?

• Are you able to answer questions customers often ask, such as:

> o Does the doctor speak my language? Will there be communication problems due to language differences?
> o How will this treatment help me? This is an elective procedure -- why do I need it?
> o Is your facility best suited to complete my treatment?
> o Is medical travel abroad safe and can I really save money?
> o Can I locate case histories and treatments performed by this doctor that are similar to mine?
> o How can I make sure an international medical facility is credible? o Can I afford this?

Creating Solutions

Developing a multi-touch approach to customer relations and patient care results in multiple benefits for your medical practice or facility. Other than face-to-face contact, the telephone is still considered the best way to reach out to prospective patients and engage in dialogues and in-depth conversations regarding healthcare or surgical procedures. Multiple avenues of communication, marketing and services are essential in this field.

Consider the benefits of a multi-touch system approach:

• Return on Investment (ROI) is higher when efforts are made to create and enhance relationships with prospective patients. Don't forget that a patient's opinion of your services will be a key to the success of your services in the future.

• Customer satisfaction is achieved through the process of a smoothly working team, not by a number of different individuals from different organizations.

• Communication with potential customers early in the buying process helps influence their expectations.

• Never, ever forget the human touch when it comes to providing health care services. Human beings are guided by emotion in most decision-making processes.

In every communication with a client or patient, emphasize the multi-touch concept. Studies have shown that effective patient acquisition strategies blend components of e-mail, Internet-based marketing, interactive media, and the human voice to achieve success in today's highly competitive medical travel environment. The multi-touch approach increases the probability of successfully landing a client by over 65%. In today's competitive marketplace, utilizing the human touch will make all the difference in the world in the success of your practice or facility.

Understanding Your Selling Value
in Price Sensitive Medical Tourism Market

How much does it cost? The one question most commonly used by medical tourism consumers that automatically leads into a low price war among medical provider in this highly competitive marketplace.

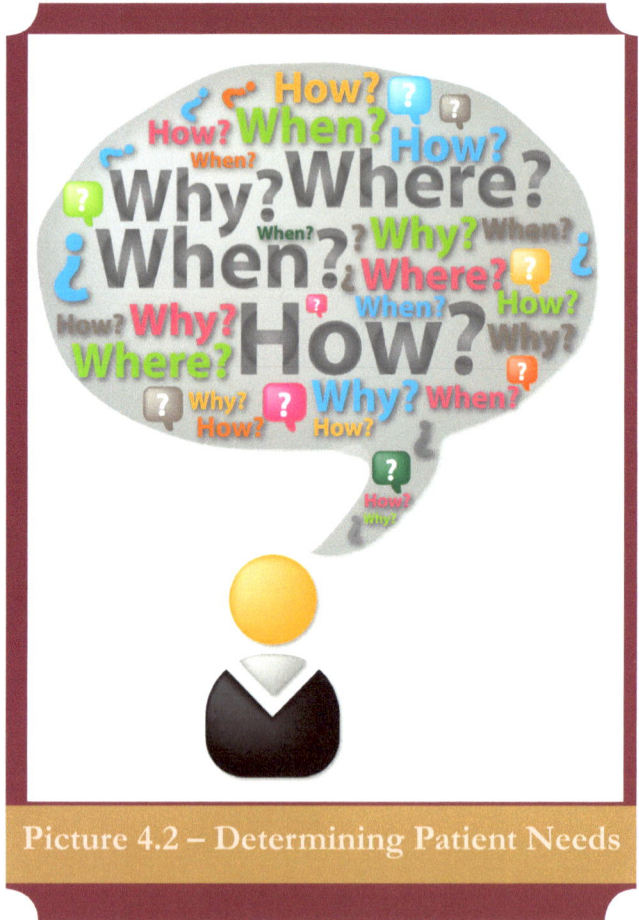

Picture 4.2 – Determining Patient Needs

Cost considerations are often at the top of the list when it comes to consumers seeking the best value for any service or product, combined with a desire for quality. Medical consumers are especially conscious of quality, results and effectiveness of medical treatments and procedures both domestically and abroad.

Still "*how much is this going to cost me?*" tends to be one of the first thing that goes through a patient's mind when she finds out she needs surgery, or he wants a nose job.

The art of selling your medical services for a higher value is understanding a key element about the medical tourism process.

Selling is all about doing the right homework up-front and attempting to get it right the first time.

Healthcare service providers need to delay that one question until other, more important issues can be discussed, which will provide a perspective patient with the information, options, and resources that result in a successful sale of products or services.

Health care providers need to realize that cost is not the only consideration that determines whether or not a consumer makes a decision regarding a facility, treatment or procedure.

However, few patients realize how much medical services cost, from laboratory tests, to equipment and technology used in a procedure, to hospitalization or follow-up care costs.

Determining Patient Need

When discussing services, products or prices with prospective patients, it's important to understand what they're looking for and what they hope to accomplish with the procedure or service. Some of the most basic questions to ask may include:

- Why do you want or need this treatment?
- What aspect of your medical care is most important?
- When do you need this procedure?
- What will happen if you don't have the procedure at this time?
- What information will you need to make a final decision?

Healthcare providers are advised to avoid falling into the "how much does it cost" scenario at the beginning of any conversation or communication with a prospective patient. First, providers need to determine the needs of the patient and match them with the products or services you or your facility offers them.

To work around that "how much does it cost" scenario at the beginning of any issue, healthcare providers can take a few proactive steps to help guide communication into learning more about the patient and his or her needs. Comments such as:

- What are your present options?
- What are your desired treatment outcomes?
- How important is quality and experience in your decision?
- Are you looking for best quality at reasonable or affordable prices, or are you only concerned with experience?
- Are you concerned regarding follow-up care, guarantees, or warranties on procedures or outcomes?

Such questions may help guide the potential patient toward understanding that cost is only a small portion of the overall care scenario. However, medical providers should also keep in mind that the longer a person takes to make up his mind about a service, the less chance you have of making a sale.

For example, studies have determined that at the advent of any selling process, providers have a 100% chance of closing the deal after first communication with the customer. If the customer calls back a second time, the chances of closing that deal decreases to about 70%. At the third or fourth communication, you may have a 50/50 chance of acquiring that patient.

Closing the Deal

In order to enhance your chances of acquiring that patient as quickly as possible, provide transparent information regarding a patient's questions and concerns. Don't minimize their concerns regarding procedures, facilities, certifications or experience.

Avoid the "how much does it cost" question at the beginning of a conversation by gently guiding the potential client into discussing his or her needs, expected outcomes and desires. Give them options. Keep the conversation going and require specific answers, which will help you determine the emotional buying needs of every client, and then deal with cost issues and options.

Negotiations and Medical Tourism

What is a negotiation and why is it important in the sellability concept?

According to Wikipedia, Negotiation is a dialog between two or more people or parties, intended to reach an understanding, resolve point of difference, or gain advantage in outcome of dialog, to produce an agreement, to bargain, to craft outcomes to satisfy various interests of two people/parties involved in the process.

In the field of medical tourism, negotiation is a compromise between patient and a provider from various aspects such as treatment plan, treatment date, duration of stay, place to stay, cost, among many others. It is critical as the patient is shopping around for similar treatment and they may be comparing services from local providers to medical tourism providers.

The negotiations in the field of medical tourism can be effective if we clearly understand the basic elements of negotiation techniques as due to cultural and language differences it could influence the outcome significantly. To attract medical tourist we have to understand consumer mindset, their behavior, the context under which the communications are occurring and overall process.

As most of the negotiations in the medical tourism industry occur over the phone, prior to medical tourist traveling to the center, it is critical to understand some of the fundamental steps of negotiations. Following are some of the negotiation techniques that have been effective:

1. Approach all patient contact as if it's an important negotiation

When you contact a patient, be prepared to negotiate. It's a very important part of every process you perform.

2. Prepare, prepare, prepare

Enter a negotiation without proper preparation and you've already lost. Start with yourself. Make sure you're clear on what you really want out of the arrangement.

Understand the prospective patient information and their specific needs properly.

Understand the patients' needs, as well as the strengths and weaknesses of their request. Understand specific requested procedures, treatments and options before contacting – have this material available to you during the discussions.

3. Be attuned to the importance of timing

Timing is important in any negotiation. Sure, you must know what to ask for. But be sensitive to when you ask for it. There are times to press ahead, and times to wait. When you are looking your best is the time to press for what you want. Beware of pushing too hard and poisoning any long-term relationship. Plot the course of your conversation in your mind before you call, it will help you organize the timing of conversation elements.

4. Buff up your active listening skills

Effective negotiators are often quiet listeners who patiently let others have the floor while they make their case. They never interrupt. Encourage the other side to talk first.

5. If you don't ask, you won't receive

This is the cornerstone of success. Plot your course, know what to ask for and schedule the patient prospect through the steps.

Example:

- What documents do I need? Ask for them and set a specific time for receiving them.

- What is the treatment patient is looking for?

- What is the patients' budget? When will the patient be prepared to pay – now, in 1 month, etc.?

- When is treatment appointment date planned for? Set a specific target date which can be adjusted as the planning phase's progress.

- Are they talking with other providers? If so, who and what have they received so far?

- Always set a specific date and time for the next conversation, then calendar it and follow through.

6. Lead the conversation

This can't be emphasized enough. Understand your immediate, long term and ultimate objective for having the conversation/negotiation with the patient. Respect their time and yours by smoothly and professionally transitioning the conversation from one objective to the next. Get 'yes' answers or acknowledgement of agreement as many times as you can during the conversation, but particularly when transitioning the topics.

7. Personality Counts

Successful negotiations sometimes depend on personality. If you can assess your prospect's personality type, you can use the most effective techniques to show them why your service or product is right for them. For instance, if a patient is skeptical, you may want to back up your claims with documented facts and successful case histories; if a patient is social, you may want to emphasize the popularity of what you're offering.

Assess your negotiation style and build flexibility in using alternative negotiation styles. Practice the negotiation techniques and skills to reach "*win win*" negotiation agreements.

Develop and exchange creative negotiation currencies other than price. Manage the phases and critical tasks of the entire negotiation process. Select and use specific negotiation tactics consistent with your operating principals.

Respond to adversarial tactics, objections and challenges with facts and choices. Plan for the outcome – the patient prospect becoming a patient.

8. Summarize an action plan

At the end of the conversation, summarize the action plan you have outlined and re-confirm the date and time of your next conversation appointment. Practicing and perfecting this step will help you organize your notes, develop future strategies and make clear to the patient what is expected of them.

9. Have fun and be enthusiastic

Of all the skill sets that a successful negotiator possesses, the ability to laugh and have fun with an otherwise potentially stressful situation is perhaps one of the most important. Patient prospects will respond in kind and be more likely to bond with you and your good natured, professional approach. It also makes your job, and their decision making process much more satisfying.

Key Drivers of Patient Lead Conversion

The key to converting a patient lead generated from all marketing and education activities hinges upon speed, processes, and most importantly persistence. What a new consumer is looking for is how fast you act to solve their problems.

The three key drivers to consider as we evaluate industry best practices:

- •SPEED: A patient lead contacted within 6 hours converts 12 times more often than ones contacted in 72 hours or later

- •PROCESS: Lead conversion is determined 38% by lead

quality and 62% by sales process.

•PERSISTENCE: For contactable leads, you have a 92% chance of making contact after 6 attempts versus only 37% on first attempt.

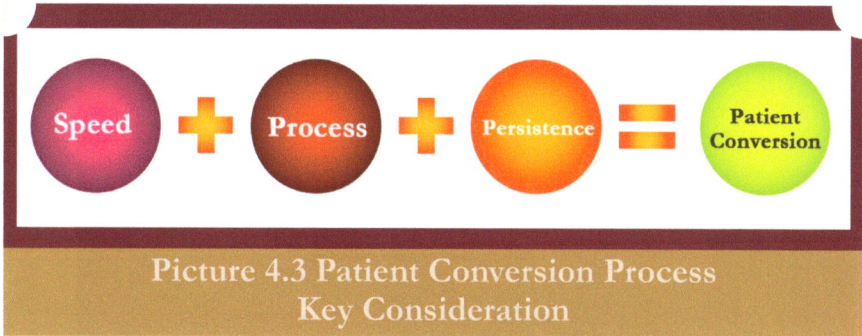

Picture 4.3 Patient Conversion Process Key Consideration

The Seven Key Rules:
Patient Qualification Criteria

When qualifying a patient lead, the best practices includes:

1. **Speed of Sales Process:** Your patient make decisions typically within 30-60 sales days.
    - o Understand specific time period when will they make a decision.
    - o Understand when they want to undergo the surgery.

2. **Number of Decision Makers:** Usually just one person makes the final decision in healthcare.
    - o Understand and document who the decision maker is in each case and see how you can communicate with the decision maker directly.

3. **Simplicity of Buying Process:** The buying process needs to be simple and straightforward with the patients doing simple research.
    - o More complexity you bring in terms of providing too many options – the more complex the buying process will become. Need to keep it very simple.
    - o Always ask for an appointment – if you do not ask – you will not get – "when can I make an appointment for you. We have limited spots and doctors schedule fills up pretty quickly"

4. **Quantity of Leads:** Generating good quantity of lead along with quality will increase the probability of converting a patient.

5. **Role of Emotion:** Emotion plays strongly and influences buying decision.
    - o This is one of the most critical aspects of whether patient decides to go with you or someone else. If you have the bond right from the first contact – your chances of success will be much higher.

o You have to understand and resonate with customer's emotional status to win them over – otherwise you are another "sales" person to them who does not understand their needs, emotions, and personal challenges.

6. **Value of Sale:** The value of the surgery should determine how much time you want to invest in a deal.

o If the ultimate value is few dollars than the efforts should reflect that – compared to higher value surgeries will require more complex understanding and negotiations.

7. **Uniformity of Offer** – The process flow should be uniform.

o In the medical tourism industry, we have to consider the market of one – i.e., each patient conversion will be unique due to needs, budgets, and desires.

Sellability –
It's all about the Customer!

As the local, regional and global competition increases, the concepts of sellability are becoming increasingly critical in medical tourism industry. One can achieve industry leadership by implementing value-based selling or customer nurturing approach. The value-based selling encourages that your customer rely on you to guide and provide authentic and reliable information.

The concept of sellability in the medical tourism industry hinges upon creating and defining ways to increase your value to your customers. Your medical tourist is looking to you for direction. You can generate value for your customer by:

- Creating a culture of cooperation and collaboration.
- Reducing chances of service 'glitches' caused by lack of clarity, communication issues and wariness of quality and excellent standards of practice.
- Creating value-based messaging that is accurately articulated to all target markets.

Educating and growing your customer base among the current and next generation of medical travelers must move toward value-based pricing and selling solutions. These are particularly important to companies offering more complex and personalized services.

Key steps to establish a value-based sellability strategy include:

- Identify your unique product offerings; what differentiates you from the competition.
- Communicate your unique solutions and services both to your employees as well as customers.
- Focus on your customer's unique needs; ask questions to identify what your customer needs to be successful.
- Align your value proposition with your customer's needs.
- Follow-up diligently to understand whether the customer needs are met or of a new solution is needed.

Chapter 5:
Profitability

Profitability means ability to gain either monetary or reputation from some type of service or venture. Sustainable profits can only be achieved once service provider can understand the links between managing customer expectations, overall total customer experience, and it's correlation with profitability of the business.

As a medical provider in the medical tourism industry, we have to find that link. We have to find a way to provide what customer needs, when they need medical attention. By doing this we will able to create sustainable profitability for the company.

In order to establish the link between profit and total customer experience, following are some of key questions that needs to be answered and measured as outcomes

Picture 5.1 Total Customer Satisfaction

- How good are your treatment results?

- How do your customers rate their treatment experiences?
- Will your customers refer your services to their friends?

To address profitability, we will discuss three key elements that are critical to business sustainability in the medical tourism industry.

- Total Customer Satisfaction
- Managing Customer Expectations
- Customer Reviews and Testimonials

In this chapter, we will discuss these three critical elements of profitability, how are they are intertwined and how they influence future customer's buying decision which will contribute towards revenues, profits, and margins. Having a delighted customer will reduce the operational cost and increase the profitability by attracting more customers.

TOTAL Customer Satisfaction

The elements of sustainable profitability in the medical health and wellness industry hinge upon **total customer satisfaction**, which includes:

1. **Availability of Distance Consultation -** You must be able to provide medical advice and consultations from a distance. This is achieved through email, Live Chats, and teleconferencing methods.

2. **Providing distance medical/health consultation before they come to you -** As you compete with local medical providers, you have to make customers feel that traveling to a different country will gain them better care and solutions to their problem. Remember that customers always have options to receive the procedure locally or anywhere in the world.

3. **Customer Service -** Customer service does not start when patient arrives in the city. It starts when the patient asks for what you can do for them at the initial point of contact. This starts from their inquiry, to discussions with a provider, and walking them through each step of the care process.

   Whether you provide customer service over the phone, via Live Chat, IM, or in person, make the process easy and seamless. This is the only way you can gain trust with the patient.

4. **Treatment Plans –** You must be able to present and provide your potential customers with a customized treatment plan.

   Are you able to provide a completely satisfactory treatment which is unique and affordable to your customers? Do you have adequate knowledge regarding safe and effective treatments plans that are currently available to your customers?

5. **International Standards –** You may have been considered as reputable surgeon in the local market, but when you're competing in the international market, you have to step up your efforts. You need to consider international certifications, international facility standards, a multi-lingual staff, and even accreditation by international accreditation organizations.

   You must be able to provide surgical excellence as well as facilities. This is expected from an international organization. Maintaining and delivering solutions that adhere and follow international standards of quality healthcare services is key to sustainable profitability

6. **Total Transparency –** You must maintain complete transparency in every aspect of your services; treatment, procedures, risks, cost, staff experience, etc.

   This is key to winning complete satisfaction. If we take the time to discuss and maintain complete and honest transparency in regard to treatments, costs, risks, etc., the patient will trust you more.

Picture 5.2 Total Customer Experience

The more trust a patient or customer feels, the more comfortable they will be, and the greater their chances of positive experiences. In turn they'll recommend your services to others.

7. **Surgical/Procedure Excellence** - When a customer needs surgery or a procedure, you must offer the best. This means providing trained, experienced and certified doctors, surgeons and support staff that is knowledgeable regarding their field, and educated in the latest procedures and technology in their field. The outcome of surgical or procedure is the critical to a profitable repeat business.

Prove that you command the superior surgical results compared to others in your field. This is achieved through contact and communication with your providers, customer feedback and testimonials and facility surveys.

Case Study

Sander is a young woman who has chosen a medical package in a foreign country for fertility treatments. The provider she contacted was patient in explaining a variety of fertility services they offered. They showed patience with Sander's questions, giving her detailed information about treatments she expressed interest in. This showed Sander that staff was experienced and knowledgeable about their field.

Sander then asked if she could communicate with the doctor that would be working directly with her. She was provided with his office phone number and email address. She chose to initiate contact with him via email and was very pleased with his fast response. They communicated several times while Sander learned more information about the procedure that would best suit her needs, as well as her doctor's experience with the procedure. This contact showed Sander not only that the doctor was accessible and able to offer her a choice of treatment plans, but that the provider company was dedicated to excellent customer service.

Sander asked staff at the facility to send her a copy of the doctor's certification and information regarding the history of the facility. She wanted to make sure the hospital and the doctor were trained and skilled in their field. The answers to her questions proved to Sander that the facility and doctor adhered to international standards of excellence and that the facility was comfortable with providing her total transparence in regard to treatments, cost, and benefits and risks of the procedure she had chosen.

This is how you generate trust with your customers.

Dealing with Expectations

Be prepared – and be able to answer questions from potential customers. Take the time to find out exactly what they're looking for. To do this, determine how they feel about several aspects or factors regarding their potential and past care.

The key to managing international patient experiences is to understand expectations and needs. Experience mapping helps develop empathy with customers and understand their increasingly complex needs. This is achieved by incorporating multiple "**touch points**" into patient acquisition strategies. The main issues involved in patient experiences are:

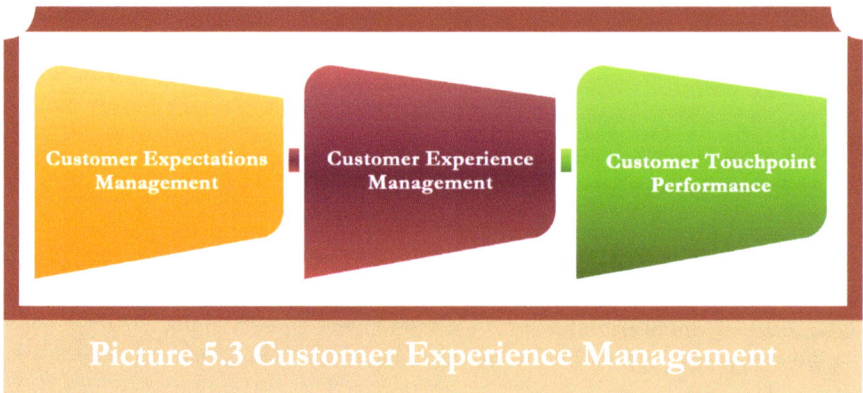

Picture 5.3 Customer Experience Management

Expectations

Are you meeting customer service expectations - what was promised vs. what was actually delivered? This is the most critical element of whether you win a customer or lose one, whether you delight a customer or customer sues you, whether a customer is satisfied enough to recommend your services to someone else, or gives poor feedback on the Internet.

Before each stage of the patient acquisition process, what does the patient expect from that stage? How are you addressing their needs as mapped for that phase of their interest?

Experience

Are you able to provide the same or better customer experience as they can receive at home? This is very important, as people traveling out of their local area have expectation of superior experience than what they can get at home. A customer's overall perceived experience will form a legacy of your credential, brand, and services. It will define who you are.

How well does your organization currently meet patient goals and experiences for each stage? Are you mapping their experience of that stage with their expectations?

Touchpoint Performance

Are you consistent and transparent at each stage of patient acquisition process to create TOTAL Customer Satisfaction? Touchpoints are defined as each point of experience that you touch the patient - e.g., initial email, initial call, describing how the treatment will be performed, treatments, procedures, aftercare, etc.

To whom do patients turn to satisfy their needs? How well do you perform key interactions with patients during the patient acquisition stages?

No matter how good your healthcare product or service is, a strong patient acquisition process is absolutely necessary for an effective and profitable business. Such a process is the voice of your healthcare business; communicating with potential customers about treatment plans as well as superlative options your center can offer them.

Many healthcare providers have perfected their skills in surgeries, treatments, or diagnosis. They fully utilize a solid group of employees, enjoy reliable suppliers, and even benefit from repeat customers. Still, many have neglected to develop a process that creates total customer satisfaction experiences from start to finish. Effective patient acquisition processes are essential to maintain and expand your international customer base.

Case Study

Jerry is a 57-year old man looking for cheaper, yet quality orthopedic surgery to repair damage done to his knee years prior. He had expectations: he wanted to be pain free; he wanted increased range of motion; and most of all, he wanted to be able to play with his grandchildren without making his condition worse.

Jerry was looking for a provider and surgeon who had the experience in the knee replacement procedure he was looking for. He had done his homework and pretty much knew that the knee replacement prosthesis he was looking for would suit him best. Of course, he was willing to listen to suggestions from the surgeon, as he realized he was not a medical expert, but Jerry also wanted the ability to give his input, and be listened to.

Jerry contacted a provider, pleased with the response from the first person he spoke to. He then contacted the doctor, and spent a week emailing and calling for additional information regarding the surgical procedure. Again, Jerry was happy. When it came time to make actual travel and accommodation arrangements, the providers helped him every step of the way. He was put in touch with a representative from the company who told him exactly what he needed for travel. The rep met him at the airport and helped him check into a hotel near the facility. At the facility, a translator helped him communicate with his nurses.

Jerry was very pleased with the results; both of the surgery and recovery process, and the help of staff in helping him accomplish his goals. They were with him, supporting him, every step of the way.

Looking for a sustainable competitive advantage? Make each customer feel like a market of one.

The new consumer behavior in this era is driven by individuality and individual needs, desires and preferences. They gravitate toward solutions that fulfill their personal needs. The customer wants - and expects - a medical provider to know and anticipate their personal preferences, and provide products and services tailored to their specific needs. Personal interaction is the most satisfying.

In order to have an impact on profitability of a medical center, the provider must know and anticipate the patient's personal preferences and provide solutions accordingly. The goal is to know each customer. Learn:

- **Their name** - Learn it and use it. Make each customer feel unique.
- **Behavior** - What type of personality are they? What are they looking for, and why? What are their expectations?
- **Treatment preference** - Are they looking for surgical or non-surgical options? Do they prefer alternative or natural medical approaches than medications and surgery options?
- **Communication preference** - Do they prefer contact by phone or email? Do they want to Skype or IM chat?

By addressing each of these, you can essentially create a 'market of one' with each and every customer.

Patient Treatment Touchpoint

This is the phase of service or product delivery that most healthcare providers are very well versed in. To ensure a quality customer service oriented business, you must consider the "bedside manners" of your staff. In addition, you must understand the cultural background of the patient, potential language barriers, and other elements that have an impact on customer service and delivery.

During this phase of the customer acquisition process must include:

- Ample communication between medical staff and customers
- Superlative care and quality in patient services
- Availability of support personnel to help address language issues, medical care follow-up and when necessary, rehabilitative services

The hoped-for result of this phase of the patient lifecycle is a happy customer ready to tell the world how great you are and offer those coveted and treasured testimonials so that others may learn and experience the same benefits from working with your organization.

Patient Reviews and Testimonials

In today's changing digital age, over 70% of the people make their buying decisions based on peer-to-peer reviews of a product and services. This segment is growing very fast. Maintaining positive customer satisfaction is increasingly a key factor of an organizational profitability.

Good customer experience as opposed to poor customer service is relative to many. Everyone's perception is different. They're the ones who control how you will be seen by the world and how people will buy your service based on their experiences.

Three outcomes drive the impact of reviews in today's world:
1. Confirmation of an original buying decision
2. A changed opinion regarding which product to buy
3. Consumer did not buy the product or service because reviews were too confusing

Case Study

Neely is a 37-year old mother of two seeking affordable treatment for her multiple sclerosis. She's not really happy with her current medical provider, or the solutions he offers to help her deal with her condition. Her insurance has been cancelled due to job loss, and her options will soon be severely limited.

Neely wants to find alternative treatments that may help relieve symptoms of her condition, but she can't afford an arm and a leg either. She's considering travel abroad, as she's heard medical tourism has grown more popular in recent years. She starts doing research on her own. She finds several providers that are potential matches to what she's looking for. She researches each of them, paying close attention to testimonials and feedback from prior clients and patients.

At the same time, Neely realizes that some facilities don't post negative or poor testimonials, so she focuses on social media such as You Tube, Facebook and Twitter to find more information regarding not only the facilities she's narrowed down, but the doctors as well. She's especially interested in video testimonials posted on social media sites, as well as independent feedback she finds on social media network pages.

These reviews provide the foundation of Neely's decision to choose one facility over another. She is personally able to contact several former patient-clients of the facility and receive unbiased, honest reviews of services before, during and after treatments.

Having access to the internet offers consumers today honest and transparent information, reviews and testimonials by former patients and clients of medical providers. In the medical tourism industry, these testimonials are worth their weight in gold.

According to research, customers shopping around and comparing services often change their mind about a service based on negative reviews, according to Marketing Pilgrim[1]. Negative feedback and reviews can devastate your efforts to provide excellent quality services to customers.

As providers, you must realize that negative information, reviews or feedback have just as much, if not more, influence on a buyer's decision making process. Where do consumers find negative feedback? You name it. Social media pages such as Facebook, Twitter, forum boards, even a provider or service website. Blogs are a powerful tool for information-gathering. Don't make the mistake of ignoring negative reviews.

Indeed, according to Marketing Charts[2] , nearly 82% of consumers make buying decisions based on reviews they've read about a service or product.

[1] Marketing Pilgrim: http://www.marketingpilgrim.com/2011/08/80-percent-of-shoppers-change-purchase-decision-based-on-negative-reviews-research.html
[2] http://www.marketingcharts.com/interactive/most-consumers-read-and-rely-on-online-reviews-companies-must-adjust-2234/deloitte-consumer-review-purchase-influencejpg/

An equal 43% either found reviews that supported their buying decision or influenced a change in their position regarding which service
or product to purchase. Nearly 10% didn't purchase anything because
they believed the reviews were either balanced between pro and con,
or complaints were so varied that the consumer decided not to 'go
there' at all.

Remember -
Profitability is directly proportionate to customer experience!

A positive customer experience is a very clear indicator for profitability - or soon to expected profitability - in cases where the customer
experience has changed from an undecided to a positive level. Negative customer feedback has a very direct impact on the number of
customers a provider may expect. Negative reviews often force a company to retain their customer base by selling services or products at a
lower price. Not only that, but you may need to increase staff support
to deal with your dissatisfied customers.

Medical Tourism
Profitability & Customer Satisfaction

Being great at what you do is about more than being a competent
professional or a skilled craftsman. It's not enough to deliver a great
product or service. It is about *the total customer experience*, from the first
encounter until the last—and everything in between.

So, putting it all together, consumers are looking for three major things
when deciding on your services:

- Customer satisfaction of prior users
- Honest and personal testimonials or reviews from previous
customers or clients
- Ability to provide services that have the greatest potential to
meet their expectations.

Your company's ability to provide these aspects of service to your customers will have a direct impact on the profitability of your company.

Picture 5.4 Sustainable Profitability

In order to achieve business sustainability we must able to execute all elements of the business. We need to find the right people, the right technology and the right management of these processes for the best in customer satisfaction.

This requires consistency in services across the board, continually updating services based on new innovations and technologies in the industry, and your ability to let your customers know that you're at the top of your game in knowing about these innovations and technologies.

As you can see, your potential for profitability rely on multiple factors of service. You must be able to show customers that you're able to give them the positive experiences they're looking for. You need to be there with your customer/patient during every step of the patient-care experience; from the moment they first contact you until they are discharged from care or aftercare services. You need to ensure a positive experience from your customers that will prompt them to tell others and recommend your services to others.

Pay equal attention to negative feedback and positive feedback. A testimonial, good or bad, provides you with a prime opportunity to learn and grow. Don't wait until negative or poor responses to your services seriously hampers your business. Nip it in the bud. Pay attention to your touchpoint services throughout the delivery process and you'll likely realize increased profits across the board.

Profitability in Medical Tourism

To conclude, there is a strong relationship between profitability, customer loyalty, customer satisfaction, and efficiency of product and/or service delivery:

- **Profit and growth** are both reliant on your customer's loyalty.
- **Loyalty** is a benefit of customer satisfaction.
- **Satisfaction** of customers is impacted by the value of services provided.
- **Value** is developed and enhanced through satisfied, loyal, and productive customer services.
- **Patient satisfaction**, in turn, is achieved through the availability of high-quality services and policies that deliver results to customers.

Each link in the chain is vital to the success of the endeavor. When one link is broken, the chain cannot bear the weight of the project. Carefully analyze each link in your chain of services to ensure that each of the points listed above provides a strong foundation for your platform. Remember: each link relies on and offers support from other links in the chain.

Chapter 6:
Medical Tourism
Infrastructure Requirements

Sustainable medical tourism business is a direct function of three critical components: People, Process and Systems. Individually, each component can represent value, but when considered together, with a framework, they can produce high value which can be sustainable and create a resilient business.

It has been observed that the medical centers integrating people, processes and systems will achieve over 50% productivity gain as well as medical travelers coming to that medical center. The next generation of medical travelers will require everything to be perfect. Partial solution to them is unacceptable. Mainstream medical travelers will seek a smooth and streamlined infrastructure and environment in order to seek medical care outside their local boundaries.

Today, more medical tourism organizations are facing chal-lenges to continue to adapt to ever changing healthcare industry. They have to become agile in reacting to market changes, medical providers have to understand their own people, business processes, and systems and how to adapt to new market conditions.

In order to establish a sustainable medical tourism program, we have to consider the medical tourism infrastructure requirements that include:

• Consumer centric programs
• Information management
• Marketing Management
• Customer relationship management

By systematically addressing and establishing an environment to address these infrastructure elements will help you manage the medical tourism business from a cottage industry type environment to a corporate sustainable market environment.

People, Process, and Systems

Sustainable medical tourism program is hinged upon three critical legs of a business. The three business components are People, Process, and Systems. To be a more resilient and agile medical tourism company, we must understand and create value in these three components. The increasing competition at local, regional and global levels along with fast changing market conditions is compelling medical tourism organizations to continuously innovate and institute an infrastructure, which would be sustainable to survive long-term.

In order to create a sustainable medical tourism infrastructure, we need to integrate people, processes and systems. The right mix of these three elements will allow us to build a resilient system, which can sustain ups and downs of the business.

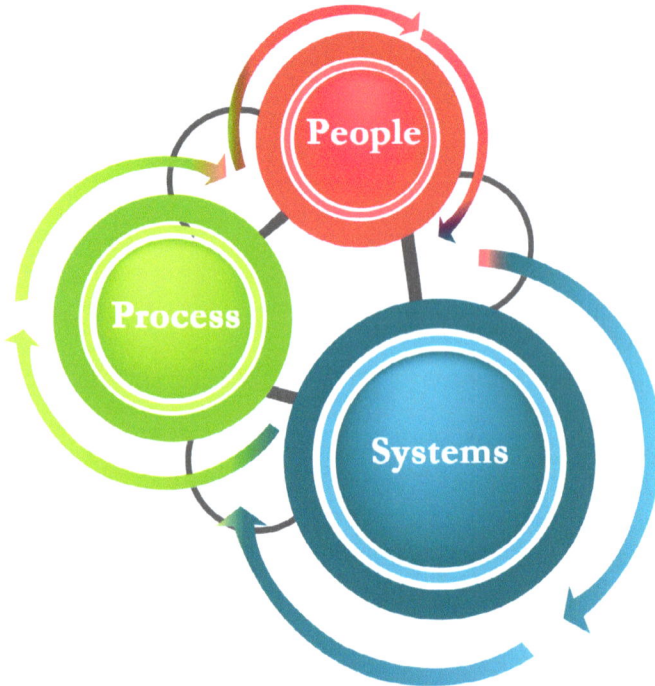

Picture 6.1 Integration of People, Processes, and Systems

People

People are the human capital, which essentially ties everything together. Human capital is the summation of what makes people valuable to our enterprise. Some of the key traits which define a human capital as valuable resource in medical tourism industry are:

- **Competencies:** Skills, Experience, Knowledge, Certification, Training, Talent
- **Behaviors**: Honesty, Integrity, Intelligence, Commitment, Balance, Drive

Human capital management is increasing becoming critical in medical tourism industry as with the rise in competition, organizations are taking, poaching or "stealing" key experienced people from other organizations based on salaries, incentives, and overall growth potential in order to gain competitive edge. Increasingly we are observing doctors, nursing staff, executives, and international patient coordinators; among others are jumping ship from one organization to the other. This is already having a significant impact as the hiring costs are increasing, training time/learning curves are increasing, overall performance and productivity is reducing, and intellectual property thefts are becoming a common place.

In addition to internal human capital issues, organizations participating in medical tourism industry are faced with a myriad of other complex people issues and challenges, especially when we are crossing and adopting cultures across local, regional and global boundaries. A vast majority of medical tourism organizations have struggled and continue to struggle to integrate right resources across its value chain.

The human capital across boundaries adds social, biological, cultural, linguistic, and psychological complexity in the medical tourism industry. The education and learning of this human capital becomes more challenging.

Many executives in medical tourism industry are realizing the overall impact, but very few are taking steps to prevent it or even know what to do in such environment.

Developing strong human capital management initiatives within an organization are essential in today's medical tourism knowledge-based industry.

The key questions medical tourism organizational experts need to ask are:

- Do you know what your key human assets really are?
- How do you know if the workforce is competent to do the tasks?
- Does your workforce have the competencies needed to move
- into a new product area, or a new market? If not, how will you get there?
- What are the competencies that are most critical to run an effective medical tourism program?
- Do you have a pool of resources locally available at affordable cost?
- Does your key resources giving you competitive edge in the marketplace?

Smart medical tourism companies are using skills and competencies of their human capital to optimize across medical tourism value networks. The skills and competencies can be mapped to link employees, contractors, channel partners, and customers across local, regional and global boundaries. The alignment of human capital across business functions is key to the success of an organization. This includes cooperation between medical tourism marketing, international patient coordination, medical experts, doctors, and overall business administration. Developing the right human capital in an organization will nourish motivation, speed, culture and other new economy imperatives. Human capital management in an organization will drive growth, retention and innovation in an organization.

Human Capital Management Elements

- Business Alignment – does your human resources aligned with your organizational needs and overall goals and objectives of medical tourism program
- Resource Planning – do you know what resources you need to run your business, what skills inventory you have?
- Resource Acquisition – how and where you will find the resources you need to fill the gap or to grow the organization?
- Resource Engagement – are people in your medical tourism program engaged and challenged to produce exemplary results?
- Resource Development – are you investing in developing, training your medical tourism related resources to be competent in their skills and behaviors to deal with international medical program?
- Resource Management – do you have right tools and management practices in place to nurture and grow the talent pool?

Picture 6.2 Human Capital Management

Benefits of Human Capital Management

As we look into the future of medical tourism industry, human capital management should be addressed as a critical element of overall sustainable medical tourism business. Human capital management planning will allow organizational benefits such as:

- Effective and efficient use of resources, when organizations can do the same amount of work with fewer staff due to reduced turnover and increased knowledge base
- Planning to understand the trends and continuity plans to weather vacancies caused by poaching or people leaving for competition
- A path for training, personal development, career counseling, and recruiting efforts
- It will allow you to attract, track and retain top talent by mapping competencies with incentives and performance

In medical tourism industry, it is no longer acceptable to just assume people will stay for a long ride, it is no longer assumed people are our most import asset. It is essential that we put processes and systems in place to retain our key assets who can provide us with competitive edge. People are critical part of medical tourism infrastructure and we need to protect, preserve and grow this talent to maintain competitive edge as well as reducing overall cost.

Process

Business Process Management in medical tourism industry relates to aligning all aspects of an organization with the wants and the needs of an international patient looking to treatment abroad. This management approach promotes business effectiveness and efficiency while seeking product innovation, business flexibility, and integration of key value chain. The key benefit of a process management is it gives us an environment under which operations can be continuously improved based on new findings while optimizing and eliminating business inefficiencies.

Similar to manufacturing, energy, or any other industry, medical tourism industry needs to establishes repeatable processes where 80% of the business can be processed through structure methodology. The remaining 20% of the business can have the flexibility to address unforeseen business situations that may arise. The basic operational value proposition of business process management is the ability to process more with less efforts and higher quality. By adopting structured processes medical tourism companies can realize three core benefits – efficiency, effectiveness, and agility.

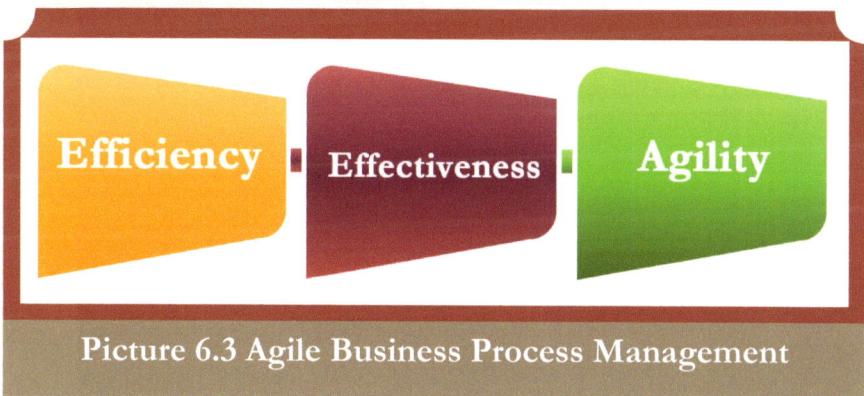

Efficiency   **Effectiveness**   **Agility**

Picture 6.3 Agile Business Process Management

Efficiency

It is very typical to see any growth oriented industry to have processes with significant waste because of manual processing, lack of coordinated efforts between departments, and a lack of ability to measure key performance indicators.

It is observed that organizations that are in process of deploying medical tourism have similar inefficiencies. By implementing a well-defined business process management methodology these wastes can be eliminated from the system which will have a positive impact on margins.

Effectiveness

Process effectiveness is initiated once you have defined initial processes and make them flow. Effectiveness will increase by analyzing information key performance indicator data and developing decision support systems to see where the processes can be fine-tuned to see greater savings and/or revenue generation. The team should able to handle process exceptions better and further control process variability. The process effectiveness in medical tourism industry also controls overall business liability and move towards regulatory compliance.

Agility

In an environment, when medical tourism is growing and evolving agility is extremely important in order to adapt to new products, markets, situations. Also medical tourism industry, being a customer service oriented business, ability to change business direction, decisions, and concepts is essential. New treatments may become available, new markets may emerge, new doctors or technology may change the rules of the game. Agility in medical tourism business can give you a competitive edge.

Benefits of Business Process Management

The business process management will allow organizations to do more with less. The process establishment forces organizations to focus on the core business fundamentals. Streamlining and aligning core business systems and processes can produce significant benefits:

• Lower your operational costs

- Enhance your customer's experience
- Boost employee satisfaction
- Improve quality in all processes
- Improved profitability
- Increased speed and customer responsiveness
- Better decision making
- Creates continuous process improvement

In the medical tourism industry business processes can be establish for each and every function. It could be in marketing, sales, operations, patient schedules, logistics, medical outcome, among many other situations. Let's review an example of medical tourism process in terms of international patient acquisition.

Patient Acquisition Process Mapping

In these tough economic times, creating a positive and lasting impression is critical to maintaining and growing your market presence. It's not the time to think only of yourself when it comes to customer satisfaction. You must clearly offer benefits to your customers.

A healthcare provider's efforts to improve customer satisfaction will fall flat if he or she only concentrates on brand satisfaction. How that brand offers beneficial products and services to clients is of utmost importance when developing the customer experience. Health providers must know what their competition is doing in order to better allocate limited resources.

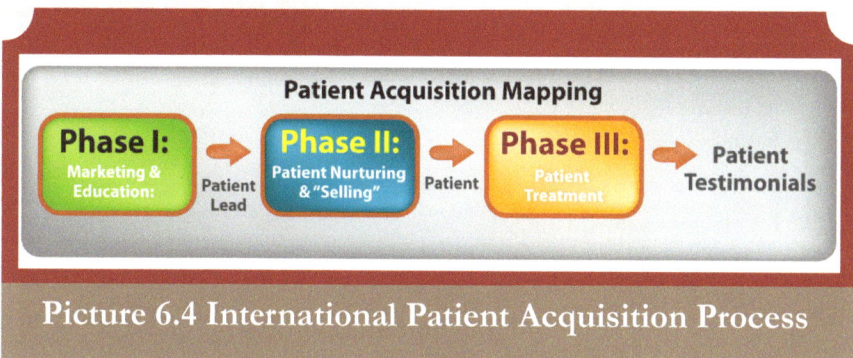

Patient Acquisition Mapping

Phase I: Marketing & Education: → Patient Lead → **Phase II:** Patient Nurturing & "Selling" → Patient → **Phase III:** Patient Treatment → Patient Testimonials

Picture 6.4 International Patient Acquisition Process

In this highly competitive medical tourism market, you must rise above the competition and create an unparalleled value proposition for your customers by integrating the complete customer acquisition process with patient experience.

Three-Phase Approach to Attracting Patients

Three primary phases are involved in attracting a patient to your center.

Phase 1: Marketing and Education

Phase 2: Patient Nurturing and "Selling"

Phase 3: Patient Treatments

Offering quality care for customers begins much before you even see a patient at your facility. In order to create total customer satisfaction, health care providers must place additional emphasis on Phase 1 and Phase 2 of the patient acquisition process rather than concentrating only on Phase 3.

Phase 1: Marketing and Education

Before a prospect becomes a patient for any healthcare facility, he or she needs to know about you, how to find you and inquire about your services. If you're not visible, they can't access your services. If you educate them about the options you provide or about your experience, and provide feedback or testimonials from patients you've treated, they'll know whether you can provide the healthcare services they need.

Spreading the word along with your success stories is one of the most effective, and important elements, to create curiosity in a medical traveler's mind, and encourages them to inquire about your services.

If they don't inquire about your services, you'll never know whether there is a market need for such services. Hence, you will be limited to your existing paradigm of serving people only in your local communities where word of mouth and proximity is their key motivator.

If done correctly, results from Phase I implementation in the patient acquisition process will result in patient leads interested in learning more about your services.

Healthcare providers need to understand the reasons for patient education and develop techniques to ensure a consistent experience. However, stakeholders in the process usually see only their own aspect of the component, rather than the entire process.

Phase 2: Patient Nurturing and Selling

Once you acquire a patient lead through effective marketing and educational approaches, you must nurture that lead. You must work hard to convince the patient that you are the best solution for him or her. Some healthcare providers mistakenly believe this aspect of healthcare doesn't rest on their shoulders. On the contrary, the best "salesperson" in an organization is the organization itself. In order to generate and maintain total customer satisfaction and quality, you, the healthcare provider, must able to control this process effectively. You must be able to offer any patient the best experience of their life.

The Importance of the Human Experience

The healthcare providers constantly deal with extreme human emotions. For that reason it is critical to nurture compassion and empathy and offer patients the expertise, information and results they're looking for in the most effective manner possible. The result of this phase is a patient that has ultimately decided to explore your services and visit your facilities.

Phase 3: Patient Treatment

This is the phase that most healthcare providers are very well versed in. To ensure a quality customer service oriented business, you must consider "bed side manners" of staff, as well as understand the cultural background of the patient, potential language barriers, and other elements. Remember that the people who touched this patient in Phase 2 of the acquisition process are different than people delivering medical services.

This phase of the customer acquisition process must include:

- Ample communication between medical staff and customers
- Superlative care and quality in patient services
- Availability of support personnel to help address language issues, medical care follow-up and when necessary, rehabilitative services

The hoped-for result of this phase of the patient lifecycle is a happy customer ready to tell the world how great you are and offer those coveted and treasured testimonials so that others may learn and experience the same benefits from working with your organization.

The 3-Phase approach creates a unique and memorable experience for your customers. You must always consider all three phases of the patient acquisition process during every aspect of your marketing endeavors. One without the other will leave a bad impression. Instead, strive to deliver a world-class product that will distinguish your services and facilities from others.

Systems

Systems are the third critical component of the business stability. Businesses involved in the medical tourism industry need to focus on the concept of using systems to effectively manage their operations. Whether it is customer relationship management system, or content management system, medical records system, or financial systems, they all need to be fully integrated with people who are managing the processes and process which they are automating to improve efficiencies.

For example, some people in the IT industry define customer relationship management (CRM) in terms of the software applications required to deal with customers. However, it is better defined as a whole business strategy – a way of thinking in which companies no longer concentrate only on their own products and services, but instead start to concentrate more on their customers in order to be more competitive. After all, without customers there would be no business or profits.

For the customers, this means the company can meet and exceed their expectations regarding exact treatment/procedure, precise and efficient service, and complete transparency.

Medical tourism companies committed to successful customer relationship must first initiate the cultural change necessary to ensure that any technology acquired can be effective. This means reorganizing the organization structure to meet the needs of the consumer/customer.

Some examples of system that can be implemented to manage business operations include:

Customer Relationship Management System (CRM)

The customer relationship management system (CRM) should be designed to follow the patient acquisition lifecycle model.

This proven and comprehensive system should be simple to operate and allow the operations management team, as well as me-dical providers, to understand and appropriately follow-up with patient requests.

The patient follow-up processes of a CRM system could have features such as patient lead management, patient information tracking, reports/ medical reports tracking and transmission, customer follow-ups, patient contact activity tracking, along with many advanced features, which will allow for smooth operations.

Content Management System (CMS)

The website development initiative should include design and development of a content management system (CMS), used to input information into the site. The CMS application will allow the medical tourism content development team to enter engaging information in the web without any technical programming support, hence giving efficiency and rapid deployment of relevant information.

This will be beneficial to maintain the site current and add continuously engaging content for the consumers to learn about new solutions and an innovation occurring in the organization as it pertains to medical travel. This is a key tool to gain productivity and manage overall reduced cost of site maintenance.

Marketing Management System

The Marketing Management Tracking System allows the marketing team to track promotional activities and where the promotions are created. This will include tracking social media accounts, forums, blogs, directory submissions, article submissions, PR submissions, as well as Meta-tag management of the system. This comprehensive system will allow the online marketing team to manage the campaigns effectively and allow control over various search engine optimization (SEO), search engine marketing (SEM), and Social Media Marketing (SMM) activities among others.

Electronic Medical Record (EMR)

An electronic medical record (EMR) system is for medical providers who deliver medical care to patients. EMR application help hospitals and physician's office to store, retrieve and modify medical records.

Following the patient through the medical care process, from point of contact to post treatment or surgical care may also require the use of electronic medical record (EMR) technology involving telemedicine, documentation and report transactions facilitation, telemedicine conferences, and long-distance pre- and post-op care offered to each and every individual patient.

An electronic medical record makes it easier to share and transfer medical information between physicians in a country of origin as well as foreign medical providers. This capability makes medical tourism easier than ever. EMRs are green, save on administration costs in tracking and filing sometimes-massive amounts of paper accumulated for patients and provide instant viewing, transmission and access to a patient record.

Not only that, but electronic records increase speed and efficiency in health care delivery options. Electronic records can be accessed through secure passwords, fingerprints and voice-activated software that increase use of telemetry, an increasingly popular mode of communication between physicians.

Electronic medical records are safer and more secure than your paper record. Computer and IT technology only gives direct access to a medical record to those qualified to view and share information. Identification systems ensure security and sharing systems ensure confidentiality. Private information is transmitted through a secure hospital system network right into the hands of the doctor who needs it and no one else.

Providers should be prepared to explain how EMRs work, and insure confidentiality in regard to data accumulation, dissemination and security of private health care records.

Technology has always been an enabler that brings efficiency to the processes and increases people productivity to high levels. The three components: people, processes, and systems together can strengthen a medical tourism program in an organization and surely give a major competitive edge over all others.

Medical Tourism Infrastructure

Infrastructure is the foundation of an organization or an initiative which is needed for the effective operations which will be necessary to function as an organization and deliver business results. In medical tourism, it can be defined as the set of interconnected pieces of the puzzle which when joined in harmony will provide a sustainable long-term impact on the growth of the business.

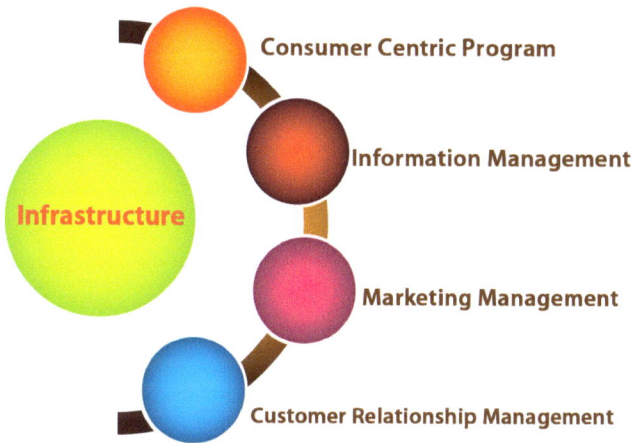

- Consumer Centric Program
- Information Management
- Infrastructure
- Marketing Management
- Customer Relationship Management

Picture 6.5 Medical Tourism Infrastructure Components

Medical tourism infrastructure consists of the following elements:

Consumer Centric Program

The consumer centric program includes everything consumer needs to research, plan and make decision for medical travel abroad. The comprehensive platform provides consumers direct access to the information they need.

For example, the program encompasses:

• Consumer centric website addressing customer needs
• Customer service oriented processes
• Unbiased, verifiable and trusted source of information

Medical tourism companies need to discover new ways to strengthen their customer's attachment to them, and maintain good relations so that the loyalty that the customers have for a medical tourism provider and its services deters them from switching to other provider.

Being truly customer-centric means taking the customer into account in every aspect of product and process. Attracting the right customers involves precise customer profiling, segmentation and marketing that is consistent across all channels, such as the direct patient leads, indirect channels (such as shops and sales partners) and the Internet. There's a distinct advantage in being customer-centric when it comes to customer interaction with your company.

Information Management

Under information management, all information whether on website or brochures or email distribution should be consistent and managed. Inconsistent information gives wrong manage to the customer and creates confusion. The information could be related to treatment and services performed, doctors' credential, pricing, pictures, videos, among many others.

Marketing Management

As one of the key element of any business is marketing, and specifically in medical tourism industry where there is a huge competition for limited supply, we need to have a very structured marketing management to create targeted demand. Tracking all marketing related activities, managing, and measuring them will be essential infrastructure project.

Customer Relationship Management

The customer relationship management is designed to follow the patient acquisition lifecycle model.

The comprehensive program should allow the operations management team, as well as medical providers, to understand and appropriately follow-up with patient requests.

Businesses involved in medical tourism needs to focus on the concept of the customer as a business asset - an asset that needs to be actively managed to get the best return on investment. Medical tourism companies can then use the information gained from their relationship with their customers to help deliver better products and personalized service, and to facilitate individualized marketing. This is necessary nowadays, when the main difference between competing companies is often nothing more than the relationship they have with their customers. Everything but the relationship can be copied from the competition.

Today, many medical tourism companies treat their customers as accounting entities - for making pure profit. The medical tourism entities must realize that the next generation of medical tourist will expect a higher quality of service than ever before. In order to meet the needs of this new generation of medical tourist, representing the main stream marketplace, a customer relationship management must be an integrated part of an enterprise solution. This should become a glue to coordinate all customer communications - phone calls, online chats, face-to-face communications, and so on.

Medical Tourism Operational Alignment

Project Management/Program Management

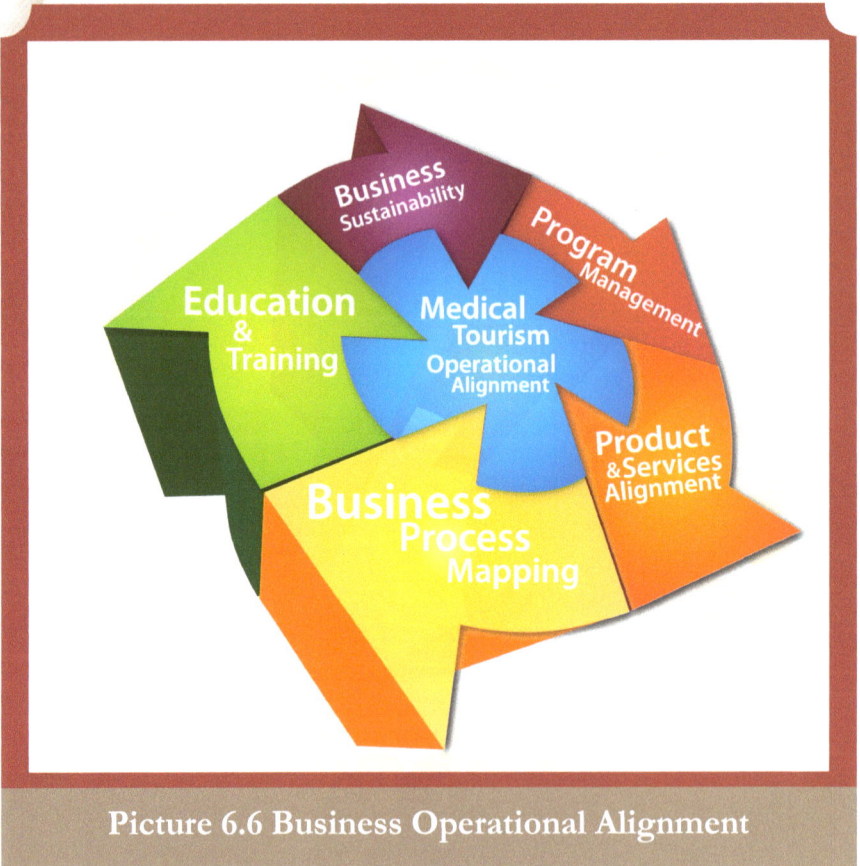

Picture 6.6 Business Operational Alignment

In the medical tourism world, as we transition from local boundaries to international boundaries several initiatives must be coordinated and management concurrently. The medical tourism operational alignment can only be met by implementing a structured Program Management initiative to manage all related projects. This will allow creating sustainable information exchange as well as solving complex cross-functional and departmental issues that arises when deploying new initiatives such as medical tourism.

In the medical tourism program management, it is essential to create a high level plan based on broad concepts and solutions for an organization. Based on this plan, each and every initiative needs to be executed in a systematic manner. Each project and task will be very well defined with an objective, action plan, strategy, process owner, and due date. The process needs to be evolutionary as each step of execution could change the direction of the medical tourism organization based on its findings and results. In order to create a resilient system, the management of this system should be based on the Progressive Performance Management system.

Progressive Performance Management can:

- Improve delivery in cost, scheduling and performance.
- Collaborate and manage expectations of external stakeholders.
- Provide competitive and high-quality services and products.
- Implement an integrated, enterprise-level business initiative.

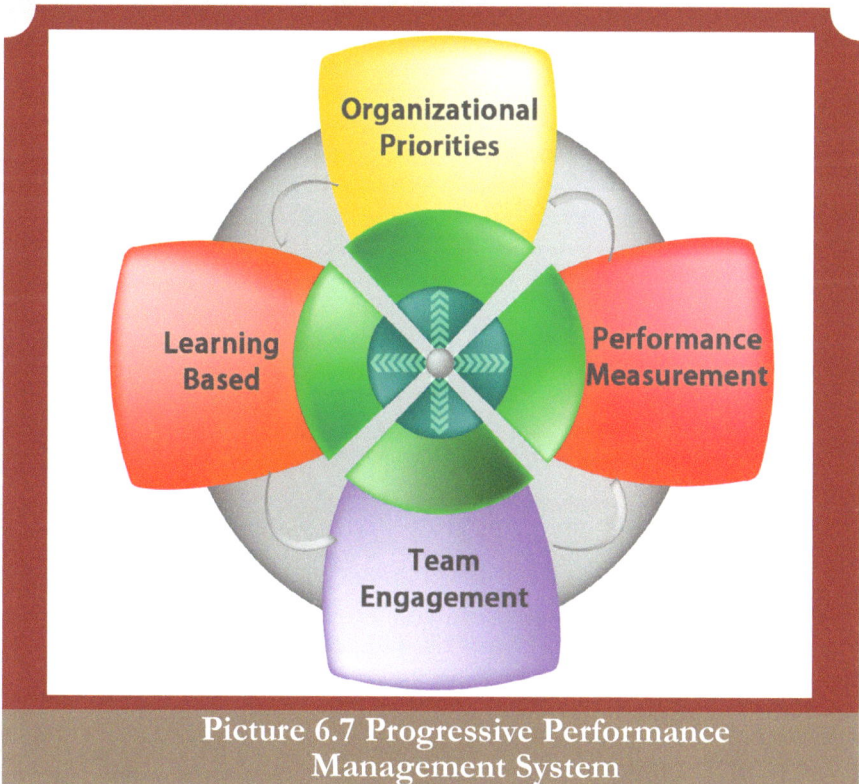

Picture 6.7 Progressive Performance Management System

- Utilize user-friendly processes and systems.
- Devise and utilize proactive techniques in program management.
- Encourage forward-thinking team or project leaders.
- Develop a staff that uses best practices to cope with changing business, technology, and customer environments.
- Design and improve processes capable of adapting to an ever-changing business environment.

The Progressive Performance Management System is a set of best practices that deal with:

Organizational Priorities: identifying which initiatives will result in best impact on the medical tourism program for the organization. By prioritizing into high, medium, low priorities, the team can manage the workload more effectively and able to accomplish more in less time.

Performance Measurement: measuring how the initiatives are progressing and changing course of the project based on lessons learned is a key element of the medical tourism ever-changing environment. To effectively manage this we not only look into hard data but also need to observe patterns. Changing an organization from opinion-based decision making to data-based decision support is the mantra.

Team Engagement: in order to gain organizational competitiveness, the medical tourism cannot be put on one's shoulder. This is a team based program which takes advantage of different skills of the team and delegate roles and responsibilities and more importantly accountability to all members of the team.

Learning Based: the medical tourism team must incorporate new industry learning to continuously improve business processes and associated task and direction of the project initiative. This would include training of the staff on new techniques, processes, and general understanding of trends and patterns.

Conclusion –
Solid Business Foundation is Key to Sustainability

While many of today's medical tourism companies are trying to differentiate themselves in the marketplace through their products and services, location, prices, several often have failed to build a business infrastructure that scales, while using company resources in an efficient manner.

A well thought-out operational plan is critical for a medical tourism organization to manage it critical resources such as finances and ensuring maximum output and long-term sustainable and scalable business infrastructure.

The infrastructure in medical tourism industry will be tied together by people, processes and systems. The essential management of infrastructure components includes factors such as policies, processes, equipment, data, human capital, and external supply chain optimization for overall effectiveness.

The medical tourism infrastructure management seeks to:

- Reduce redundancy
- Ensure standards and best practices are followed
- Enhance the information flow through the entire process
- Promote adaption in a changing environment
- Ensure organizational program management and coordination with supply chains
- Develop management policies and procedures adaptable to changing market needs

Build a medical tourism infrastructure that will support you for your long-term sustainability and not just immediate returns. Long-term an organization can build bigger businesses and grow and be recognized brand in this crowded medical tourism market.

Chapter 7:
Entrepreneurs vs. Intrapreneurs
in Medical Tourism

It's not the strongest of the species that survives, nor the most intelligent, but the one most responsive to change. ~ Charles Darwin

Overview

Do you remember the movie line, *"if you build it, they will come"*? This may work for Hollywood, but it isn't very effective in real life. When starting up any business, small or large, establishing best practices, strategies, business growth and development are essential for success.

The medical tourism industry so far been propelled by entrepreneurs or intrapreneurs. The global evolution of medical tourism has been credited to behavior and characteristics of individuals who have been pioneers to make it into an industry.

If you don't know the difference between entrepreneurs and intrapreneurs, it's time to learn. Entrepreneurship is defined as a person who creates a business or a company. An entrepreneur also raises money, makes money and saves money.

An intrapreneur is someone who works within a company (an employee) who are allowed to become corporate entrepreneurs or intrapreneurs within a specific company, firm or business. More specifically, and intrapreneurs is an employee who is able to utilize his or her own creative or innovative ideas to help the employer's company grow, add services, or develop products that benefit the business. This is done with the encouragement and support of the business owner.

Studies have shown that individuals who have a greater stake in a company or business is a more loyal and dedicated employee.

The relationship between business owners, managers and intra-preneurs creates a win-win relationship for employees and the employer. Intrapreneurship has been around for years, and major companies promoted, including GE, Toyota, Google, and Yahoo. In this chapter, we will learn more about how entrepreneurs and intrapreneurs can take this industry to next level and how you can play a role in this evolution. We will also discuss some of the essential tools of entrepreneurs such as business plans.

Entrepreneurship

An entrepreneur is defined as someone who creates businesses and companies, raises, makes and saves money. Some of the basic approaches that any entrepreneur should take in the creation of a new business include:

- Find services and products that are attractive to potential clients and customers
- Finance growth
- Develop a brand name and presence in the industry
- Maximize business or company's brand value
- Create partnerships that help provide added opportunities, profits and increase your customer base

Experts will say that entrepreneurs should focus on ten basic aspects of their new business during the first six months of the creation of such a business. In the field of medical tourism, this is especially important. For example:

- Develop a concept and develop a business model that suits your medical tourism company and client needs and has a unique value proposition
- Find business partners, investors and lenders in the medical field - this means independent doctors and surgeons, outpatient facilities, clinics and hospitals
- Create a brand to enhance your marketability and effective selling endeavors

- Brainstorm methods to increase your revenue resources

Of course, there's much more involved in entrepreneurship, such as recognizing opportunities, taking the time to analyze costs and benefits, determining your sales and marketing approach, anticipating your ROI and of course, competition and supply and demand for your medical tourism resources and business endeavors.

Intrapreneurship

Intrapreneurship allows the business' employees to become intrapreneurs or corporate entrepreneurs within a specific business or firm. In this way, employees are able to utilize their own innovative and creative ideas to help their employer grow, enhance or add services and products to the business. This is done with the full backing and encouragement of the business owner.

Careful research and studies have determined that the best way to encourage employees to stick with the company as well as to promote loyalty, ingenuity and creativity is to offer them a stake in the business.

The basic goal of encouraging intrapreneurship is to create loyal and dedicated employees. Business owners and managers willing to take advantage of other ideas and resources create a win-win relationship between both employer and employee -- hence an employee/intrapreneur.

Let's Talk about Intrapreneurship

How do you Create an Intrapreneurship Program?

Encourage team-based environments in your medical tourism company. Give your employees access to and the freedom to become a part of your team. Your employees may offer a wide range of experience, ideas, contacts and motivation that many business owners overlook due to the "traditional" employer/employee relationship in the workplace.

- Set up meetings or conferences among employees for ideas on how to improve services, products and processes.
- Let your employees read and comment on your marketing and sales plan.
- Determine various targets and milestones that the company may aim for both short-term and long-term planning

Managers and business owners who dare to allow employees to take the initiative in many aspects of the development of a medical tourism organization increases creativity and innovation and enhances profitable ventures, especially when everyone in the organization is working toward and reaps the benefits of the goals of that organization.

Conclusion

The saying, "no man is an island" is as true in business as it is in other environments. Business owners, especially those in the fast-pace and quickly-growing field of medical tourism will find that working together as a team benefits not only business owners, but employees.

Intrapreneurship has grown in both concept and practice in major corporations around the world. Don't be left behind. No matter how big, or small, your business, it can benefit from the advantages of intrapreneurship.

Strategic Business Planning for Medical Tourism

Not all business plans are created equal. A strategic business plan designed to fit the goals of hospitals and clinics trying to attract international patients is different than a plan for opening a local hospital or clinic for local patients. While many of the basic points are similar, those in the medical tourism field must be able to recognize the special needs, concerns, and demands of medical travel when it comes to providing optimal medical care.

Why Business Planning for Medical Tourism?

When it comes to establishing a progressive medical tourism company, you need to establish a method that helps identify, study and analyze various factors that are vital for the success of any business based on changing economic and social environment. In the medical tourism business, that means increasing performance, and developing and deploying interventions that help keep your medical tourism business on track.

Some of the greatest benefits of using the progressive solutions include but are not limited to:

- A decision making tool that integrates strategic business planning with key performance indicators
- Increases inter- and intra- enterprise collaboration
- Identifies key data requirements to make critical decisions and manage business, budgets, and resources effectively
- Creates resilient yet structured environments to address rapid evolution of business and technology
- Resolves conflicts between inter- and intra-enterprise goals by bridging gaps
- Captures critical organizational requirements
- Coherent and sustainable models for leveraging business outcomes

Progressive Solutions for the Medical Tourism Industry

To start customizing a strategic business plan particularly geared to the needs of the medical tourism industry, business developers need to keep important key factors uppermost in their minds. These include:

- Identify your vision
- Establish your mission
- Identify your vision
- Establish your mission
- Determine your objectives
- Prescribe strategies for success
- Create action plans

This may seem elementary, but it's amazing how many individuals in the medical industry fail to establish these basic points in their strategic marketing plans, especially those involving the medical tourism business.

Medical tourism industry providers must be able to plainly state their

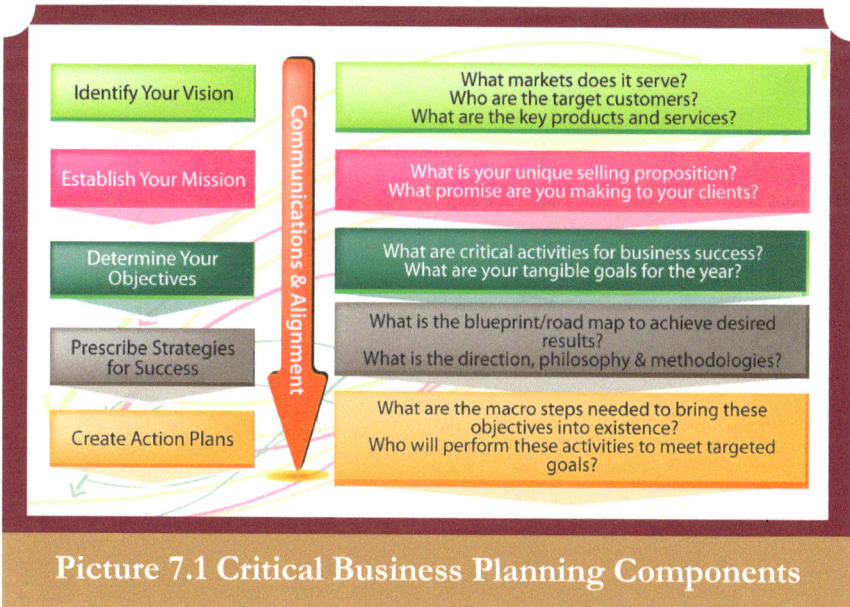

Picture 7.1 Critical Business Planning Components

objectives, visions, and mission to enable the creation of adequate and effective strategies throughout the organization. Such key points help business planners to determine viable and functional actions as well as performance metrics.

Unfortunately, a great many strategic business plans are also too complex and don't offer clear visions or goals in any of the above listed factors. What you're left with is an ill-defined plan that only offers general guidelines and not specific point-by-point, strategic marketing plans that help increase the growth, development and success of your medical tourism business.

In order to create a compelling and realistic executable plan you must consider the following points.

Vision Statements answer these questions:

• What type of company is it?
• What type or demographic market does it serve?
• What is its geographic range or scope?
• Who are targeted clients or customers?
• What are the main services and products?
• How do you envision growth or size of your company?
• What are the potential earnings or revenue of the company?
• How many patients/employees will your company be able to serve?

Mission Statements answer these questions:

• Why does your company or business exist?
• What is your company's unique selling proposition?
• What services or products are you committed to offering customers?
• What type of promises are you making to customers?
• What needs or problems do our services or products resolve?

Objectives should address these factors:

• Create objectives that can be graphed
• Give every objective a numerical value
• Define what aspects are vital to business success

- Provide quantifiable pulse of the business
- Focus resources toward specific results
- Establish a framework for accountability and incentive pay

Strategies consider these factors:

- A blueprint/roadmap for building and managing the business
- Set the direction, philosophy, values, methodologies
- Define the business model
- Establish a method for decision evaluation
- Set limits on what a company/department will do or will not do

Action Plans consider these factors:

- Assign target completion dates in order to assure accountability
- Define specific actions to be undertaken
- Limited to business building or infrastructure projects
- Related to specific strategies or objectives
- Never list "job description task"
- Schedule by quarter

Summary

Briefly, a progressive medical tourism solution forces you to identify your vision - what are you trying to build or create? Your mission statement and goals should explain why your business exists in the first place. Determining what measurable success factors will target your ultimate objectives and identifying strategies to get there will explain how you intend to succeed in the medical tourism business. Most importantly, a strategic business plan must outline the work that needs to be done, a schedule for its completion, and a determination of who is going to be assigned to complete various tasks and assignments to help your business reach its goal.

Translating your strategy into positive performance for the organization means keeping your goals and strategy plans simple and firm. It also means using language that everyone understands and the ability to identify priorities and stick to them.

Creating a strategic business plan for hospitals and clinics for use within the medical tourism industry will help to create teams who know their jobs, like their jobs, and perform at optimal levels. It also means informing your staff and employees of exactly what is expected in no uncertain terms, as well as creating a working environment that creates cohesive and patient-based care and concern. A strategic business plan enables everyone within the organization from top to bottom levels to become part of a successful team of healthcare providers whose focus is to optimize and continually improve quality and service.

Characteristics of Medical Tourism Entrepreneurial Success

Why do some entrepreneurs become successful while others are unable to take their companies to the next level? What characteristics an entrepreneur should possess to succeed in medical tourism industry? Let's look at some of the success factors that are most critical in this business:

Take Action: there is lot of talk and hype in medical tourism industry. Few people are able to separate facts vs. fiction. The best way to address this is to learn about the factual information, data, patterns to determine the actions one needs to take and not getting into the trap of fiction.

Knowledge and Skills: understanding the medical tourism and the specific market needs is critical. It is commonly observed that due to several misinformation, or lack of any credible source of authentic knowledge base, several entrepreneurs are misled. Gaining right knowledge base is critical to success. Knowledge coupled with understanding their own skills inventory, their personal strengths and weaknesses will help make the right hiring decision to fill the competency gaps.

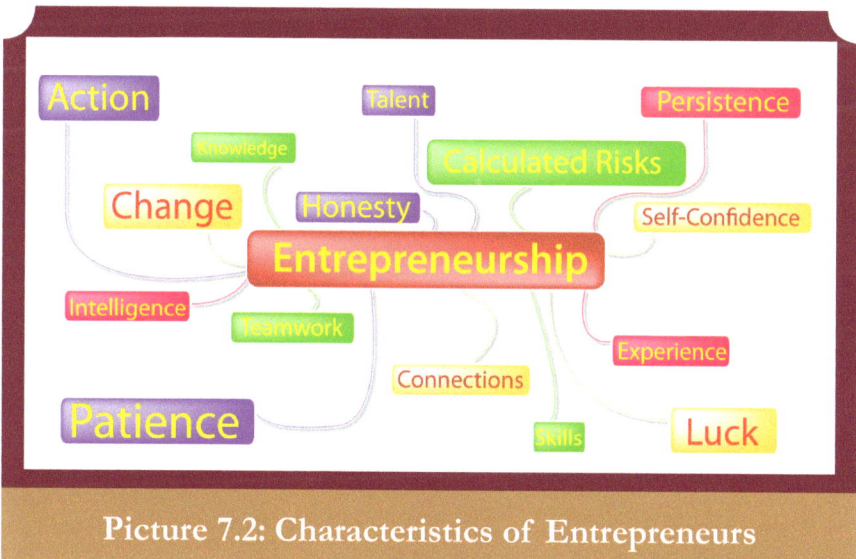

Picture 7.2: Characteristics of Entrepreneurs

Creativity and Talent: out-of-box thinking, innovation of process, continuous improvement initiatives will help create a unique solution rather than a "me too" product which is harder to sell and differentiate in the market.

Intelligence and Self Confidence: the common sense, ability to solve problems, performing situation analysis will able to help them with presence of mind and solving many situation proactively. Intelligence coupled with self-confidence is important to be sure of the path you are on – otherwise second-guessing your own assumptions would pull you back.

Patience and Persistence: in medical tourism, like in any other industry, patience is the key factor. You cannot give up after first failure, or second or third. From each failures and successes we have to come out with lessons learned and develop continuous improvement initiatives. Persistence is a major characteristics which allows entrepreneurs to continue pressing forward despite failures.

Teamwork: one of most important trait in the entrepreneur world is collecting the right team with complementary skills to execute the business plan established. The team should be composed of not necessarily like-minded people as they may not able to challenge false theories and remain in agreement that may lead them towards wrong road.

Experience and Risk Management: it is one of the most important characteristics of an entrepreneur is the ability to take risks for a higher reward. Most successful entrepreneurs have taken calculated risks which limit their financial and legal exposure.

Luck: last but not least, luck is a major factor in a successful entrepreneur world. People often find the right solution at the right time accidentally!

Entrepreneurs are known for execution. Without execution, people just talk and take no action. Hence, they are unable to engage in the process and learn which is a correct path and how they can influence the outcome of that path.

Creating your own future, controlling your own destiny is what an entrepreneur does. Taking actions, making things happen is what they thrive on!

Conclusion

Entrepreneurship and intrapreneuership is the key to understand and use some of the characteristics to propel the medical tourism industry into next generation. As medical tourism industry goes into mainstream market, the entrepreneurial spirit will be a key factor towards innovating and diversifying the products and services.

Entrepreneurship will always be driving force towards new ventures, whether it is vertical integration of the medical tourism industry or a horizontal one. More entrepreneurs with different cultural background will establish the next wave of medical tourism.

Medical tourism will benefit from entrepreneurs able to break away from myths, industry noise and false expectations, and understand the fundamentals of the business. As we know, ninety percent of start-up businesses fail in first year. It's critical for people (entrepreneurs) and organizations (intrapreneurs) entering the medical tourism industry to understand the basics of actionable plans and execution strategies.

Afterword

The medical tourism industry is going through a major transformation. It is moving from an early adopter marketplace to a mainstream market. The consumer behavior in this market demands maturity of the medical tourism product. In order to survive in this market, the medical provider must move from being a cottage industry to mature organization with structured infrastructure.

The medical tourism industry is also currently viewed very narrowly with respect to meeting patient's medical needs across borders. As the industry matures, we have to consider all related services including pharmaceuticals, medical equipment manufacturing, human resources, training and qualifications, clinical trials, among many other aspects of the industry. The impact of this industry will be far superior that when manufacturing or IT industry became global. The impact on each economies dealing in the healthcare sector would be much greater than what we could imagine.

In order to reach a critical mass in the industry, we have to increase the awareness and education to propel the demand. We have growing supply across the world. But the demand has not kept up proportionally with the supply. Defining and learning about characteristics of market leaders will help organizations learn about their specific customer value proposition. We need to learn what motivates new mainstream consumers.

Understanding supply chain and establishing sustainable infrastructure are essential to determine how the demand will help in developing sustainable business practices.

References:

Crossing the Chasm: Marketing and Selling Disruptive Products to Mainstream Customers by Geoffrey A. Moore

The Discipline of Market Leaders: Choose Your Customers, Narrow Your Focus, Dominate Your Market by Michael Treacy and Fred Wiersema

PlacidWay

PlacidWay, a U.S.-based medical tourism company, is the ultimate internet resource for the medical, health and wellness tourism industry.

PlacidWay helps medical centers improve top-line performance, enhance competitive position, and achieve the most productive organizational alignment among people, processes, and systems. PlacidWay opens the door to an entire world of the finest in medical and wellness programs, presenting top experts in critical care, cosmetic procedures, complementary and alternative medicine, and medical spa retreats. Differentiate yourself in this highly competitive medical tourism market and gain competitive edge through PlacidWay.

PlacidWay is designed for consumers who place a premium on their quality of life. Whether they have a physiological need requiring medical attention, a social motivation to change the way they look, or an inherent desire to seek self-actualization through organic, holistic, and healthy healthcare options, PlacidWay provides enormous options.

PlacidWay is a place where consumers begin their journey toward greater health, balance, and total well-being. Consumers are given a complete freedom to choose their own treatment at their own choice of medical center or facility, and in a country of their choice.

PlacidWay is an internationally acclaimed medical tourism company helping healthcare providers enhance their competitive positioning while improving top line performance and achieving the most productive organizational alignment among people, processes, and systems.

PlacidWay combines a value-based approach with real-world expertise and client-centric culture to create, build, and deliver outstanding solutions that give customer a competitive advantage.

Differentiate yourself in this highly competitive medical tourism market.

PlacidWay Contact Information:
PlacidWay
Phone: +1.303.500.3821
Email: info@placidway.com
Websites:
www.placidway.com
www.placidsolutions.com
www.placidblog.com